ABORTION AND THE POLITICS OF PREGNANCY

THE BATTLES BETWEEN PRO-LIFE AND PRO-CHOICE, THE RED STATES AND THE BLUE STATES, AND ROE V. WADE AND DOBBS V. JACKSON

KEITH AND ELIZABETH PORTER

ON-THE-SIDE VENTURES

We want to thank you for taking the time to read our book. Whether you are pro-life or pro-choice, please take the time to leave a review on the basis of the writing, not on your personal preference of the idea of abortion. We worked very hard to compile the *history* of abortion in the US and we would appreciate any reviews that we can get. You can leave a review by clicking the link below (if you are on an ebook) or by scanning the QR code with your phone (if you are using a print version). The first 100 people to leave reviews will get their choice of one free paperback copy of this book or one free copy of any other book I have previously published or will publish in the coming months. All you need to do is email me with a screenshot of your review at porter62185@gmail.com and I will reach out to you to get your desired selection.

https//tinyurl.com/abortionpaperback

CONTENTS

Introduction   1

1. In Each Corner   11

2. Contextualizing Abortion Before 1973   43

3. Roe v. Wade   77

4. Abortion Data and Law Post-1973   97

5. Supreme Court Decision 2022   128

6. Impact and Fallout   143

Conclusion   158

References   162

Trigger Warning: Abortion is a difficult topic and tends to emote passion. There are no graphic descriptions, but the topic is heavily discussed and analyzed. Our goal is to present this book from a neutral viewpoint that gives the information and arguments without choosing a side.

INTRODUCTION

In a touching letter written by 'H' in Harvey-Jenner (2014), a young woman lovingly explains her predicament to the fetus she will not be able to carry to full term.

Little Thing:

> I can feel you in there. I've got twice the appetite and half the energy. It breaks my heart that I don't feel the enchantment that I'm supposed to feel. I am both sorry and not sorry.

> I am sorry that this is goodbye. I'm sad that I'll never get to meet you. You could

have your father's eyes and my nose and we could make our own traditions, be a family. But, Little Thing, we will meet again. I promise that the next time I see that little blue plus, the next time you are in the same reality as me, I will be ready for you.

Little Thing, I want you to be happy. More than I want good things for myself, I want the best things for the future. That's why I can't be your mother right now. I am still growing myself. It wouldn't be fair to bring a new life into a world where I am still haunted by ghosts of the life I've lived. I want you to have all the things I didn't have when I was a child. I want you to be better than I ever was and more magnificent than I ever could be. I can't do to you what was done to me: Plant a seed made of love and spontaneity into a garden, and hope that it will grow on only dreams. Love and spontaneity are beautiful, but they have little merit. And while I have plenty of dreams to go around, dreams are not an effective enough tool for you to build a better tomorrow. I can't bring you here. Not like this.

I love you, Little Thing, and I wish the circumstances were different. I promise I will see you again, and next time, you can call me Mom.

In the heated exchanges between pro-life and pro-choice camps, there seems to be an objectification of woman as a vessel, rather than an acknowledgment that she is a unique person who may have experienced a soul-shattering life of hardships and trials that sculpted her into her present self. This letter speaks for that young girl or woman who has to confront the reality that she is pregnant with a little one who she cannot allow to grow to full-term for whatever reason. She is a person who needs to think whether she has the long-term physical, mental, or emotional capacity to be in it for the great responsibility of being a mother. Most pro-choice advocates align themselves with this type of thinking which is tied to what is best for the mother's physical, mental, and emotional well-being. One woman shares her story (Brand, 2022):

Even being in my 60s, my abortion remains the single greatest regret of my life, which has caused me immeasurable grief. Some years have been more difficult than others to weather the storm of emotions. For the most part, I've found peace, however, grief and regret lurk always just beneath the surface. Young and unable to recognize the enormity of my decision, I made a cavalier, impulsive choice. How I wish–oh, how I wish–I had been unable to make that choice.

Again, it is important to take note that this is a real person. Her experience is authentic and a reality that many women who have had abortions likely experienced. As much as pro-choice advocates try to diminish this pain and trauma, it is a reality. The woman who lies on that table in the clinic, willingly giving her consent to abort an already living being inside of her, is not an automaton; she is a person with feelings and regrets she will inevitably carry throughout her life. The pro-life camp would like to alleviate this woman's pain, but ultimately it is the individual's right to decide for herself.

The ongoing debate on abortion leads us to a moral stalemate between personal freedom and the laws of the land. It is an ethical quagmire dominated by hidden patriarchy, society, religion, ethics, politics, morality, and questions about what constitutes life. The recent Supreme Court overturning of the Roe v. Wade case has completely divided America into two opposing camps. Whether you like it or not, you are expected to have an opinion. It does not matter where in the world you live, social media has been abuzz with pro-life and pro-choice posts. It's easy to comment on these issues without much knowledge about the complexities involved. Unfortunately, there are many people who offer a viewpoint without doing their homework, because they have been influenced by their families, churches, schools, colleges, and universities. Men are allowed to have an opinion on an issue that deals solely with the body of a woman. Public polarization about the issue of abortion begs a clearer understanding of the relevant points of view and how they were seeded.

Sexual intercourse has become a rather complex and complicated act in its own right. With the advances in science and in-vitro fertilization, and the differentiation of sexual orientation, it doesn't necessarily entail a shared experience between a man and a woman. At the end of the day, it is solely the body of a woman—whatever pronouns (she/her/they/them) that the body chooses to use—who bears the possibility of parturition. Pregnancy can be a privilege and a burden, depending on your perspective. For the purpose of this book, we will refer to women as she or her, with no disrespect intended to those identifying by other pronouns.

To begin, let us understand the fundamental difference between pro-choice and pro-life stances.

Pro-choice

A girl of 10, raped and abused by a relative, finds herself pregnant. Is she compelled to carry the seed of this violent act to its end? A woman living in the developing world finds herself pregnant with her fifth child while living in abject poverty with no food or place to live. Is she expected to carry this baby to term and have it perish anyway due to malnutrition? Pro-choice advocates would assert that under these circumstances, the 10-year-old girl or the woman from the developing world has the right to choose whether they proceed with their respective pregnancies. Pro-choice believes that it is the female's prerogative to decide what is best for herself and her body.

Pro-life

When the sperm of a human male reaches the egg in the ampulla of the fallopian tube of a human female, a zygote cell is created. Is this zygote a living being that has rights? Or do the rights of the host supersede the rights of the zygote? Pro-life advocates would debate whether the point of conception makes this zygote a viable human entity worthy of having its own rights equal or even more important than its mother. Pro-life advocates believe at the time of conception, the zygote becomes a viable human being and has the same right to freedom as the mother host. The termination of this life is akin to murder.

Both of these viewpoints are embedded in a worldview informed by multiple factors: your geographic location, level of education, social, cultural, and religious upbringing, gender, and your life experiences. No matter which stance you take, your viewpoint has validity because it is based on your worldview, but it's important to understand the historical perspective that brought us to this juncture.

As one of the largest democracies in the world, the United States of America sets the benchmark for the handling of human rights issues, and its best practices resonate around the world—including the abortion debate. The world was relatively silent around the abortion issue until the Roe v. Wade verdict was publicized in Texas on January 22, 1973. The Supreme Court issued a decision citing the Due Process Clause of the Fourteenth Amendment of the United States Constitution, which states that Roe had a "right to privacy" and thus the courts protected her right to an abortion. In one fell swoop, the world changed for many decades, and this ruling sent a ripple effect on abortion laws across many countries of the world.

Since 1973, there has been a move toward liberalization of the abortion issue in the more developed countries of the world. Development entailed changes in the roles of women in these countries, and laws began to change to acknowledge women as equal partners in the home and workplace. As a result, women became a crucial part of the labor market and this changed the dynamics around pregnancy, family planning, and childcare.

According to the Population Resource Bureau (2021), "an estimated 56 million abortions occurred each year from 2010 to 2014, and nearly half of those—25 million—were considered to be unsafe." Most unsafe abortions take place in the developing regions of the world where 13% of deaths related to pregnancy and childbirth are due to unsafe abortions, while seven million women have to be treated for complications caused by unsafe abortions.

In Africa, it is estimated that eight million abortions occur each year, and three-quarters of them are believed to be unsafe. African women are more likely to live in countries where abortion is illegal. In 2017, there were 15,000 abortion-related deaths among African women mainly in countries where abortion is illegal.

In Asia, there were 39.4 million abortions between 2010 and 2014, and 42% of these were unsafe. In Latin America and the Caribbean, there were 6.5 million abortions between 2010 and 2014 with 76% being unsafe. The evident trend from these statistics is that unsafe abortions conducted under dangerous, unhygienic conditions are responsible for a large percentage of the mortality rate of young women in the developing world.

When we compare the developing world statistics to North America, it's apparent there is a direct correlation between legalizing abortion and mortality rates of young women. North America recorded 1.2 million abortions between 2010 and 2014, but only 0.9 percent of these were unsafe. In Europe, 4.3 million abortions were recorded in the same time frame with only 11% unsafe abortions.

We can conclude from these statistics that when women are denied the right to a self-determining choice about their bodies, it does not stop them from desperately seeking illegal solutions that could jeopardize their health and well-being and condemn them to premature death.

America is in the midst of a moral and legal time-bomb. The country is dominated by a Christian majority who have drawn the lines in the sand–they will not sanction abortions in any situation. The United States has the largest Catholic and Protestant population compared to any other country in the world, with approximately 250 million, and many in these groups are opposed to the deliberate termination of a pregnancy. According to these churches, abortions violate the rights of the fetus, because it is linked to their belief in life as sacred—deliberately killing a potentially viable being is considered murder. Christians believe only God can give life and end a life. They also believe that legalizing abortion promotes fornication and expands questionable morals, while condoning the brutal act of killing an unborn fetus.

The question remains: Will change in the law prevent abortions, or does it push the act underground where unsafe practices could lead to an increase in female mortality?

In Each Corner

The metaphor of two boxers going at it in the boxing ring is the perfect way to view the debate on pro- and anti-abortion stances. If you have been following the debates raging since 1973 Roe v. Wade, you would undoubtedly call it a fight with unlimited rounds. In fact, we could take it further and call it an endless war that will never see a resolution, because at the heart of the debate on abortion is human life and morality.

To understand abortion, it's important to acknowledge this is an act that really affects females only. Her body is the only vessel that can support, carry, and nurture new life. Almost every young girl is brought up in an environment—whether it's a supportive or dysfunctional family, or as a custodian of the state—with basic moral values and principles that prepare her for the adult world.

The reality is not always as simple as it's made out to be in the movies. Real life is messy and rough. You don't always meet your knight in shining armor, marry, and ride off into the sunset to live happily ever after. This is the fairytale lie that most females are fed growing up. In real life, you could fall in love with an absolute miscreant whose only intention could be to get you in the sack. In real life, you could have your drink spiked and find yourself the victim of rape. In real life, you could have had sex for the first time at 14 and had no idea that babies were made that way.

Females carry the burden of responsibility for the entire human race within their wombs. It's both a noble and burdensome obligation. Having a uterus does not necessarily make you a wonderful mother. You may have the tools, but that does not mean you possess the skills to construct a house.

As a young female, you may be brought up as a Christian, Muslim, Hindu, or Jew, and you faithfully believe in the sanctity of life and no sex before marriage—but life will often throw you curveballs. Imagine this scenario: You are ready to start college, you have sex with your boyfriend, and the condom breaks. A pregnancy at this time of your life is just not an option. Your religious morals and values haunt you. You stand at a crossroads and you have to choose. Throw away your plans and dreams for a future, and give it all up to have a baby or choose abortion and the prospect of a better life. You are now left to make the right decision. Is there such a thing as making the *right* decision?

Morality

Making the right decision is based on morality and the idea that there is such a thing as absolute right and wrong actions, but in reality, morality does not truly exist. It is a shared belief, a set of values that a group of people agrees to uphold. Most of these beliefs were passed down through history and culture as the human race evolved. Morality becomes problematic when our personal sense of morality does not line up with the society we live in.

Morality comes with an emotional undertone and a sense of bias, based on a range of factors that have collided to make you who you are and what you stand for. If you grew up in America's South with parents who supported the Republican Party and stood for white middle-class morals and values, you'd most likely be pro-life. If you grew up with a liberal family in the North whose beliefs were more aligned with democracy and civil rights, your sense of morality may be pro-choice. Even this is not cast in stone because your values are fluid and can be influenced by a range of factors. The human psyche is composed of layers of thoughts and experiences washed over by

emotions. Our sense of morality dictates our emotional response to events and situations.

What we must not forget is that morality is not a fact; it is more an opinion based on the circumstances of your life. Our morality drives our emotional response and the stances we take on issues in the world such as abortion, the death penalty, the LGBTQI community, racism, feminism, suicide bombers, and mass shootings at schools. When you embrace the idea that your morality is not based on some fixed truth, you realize that a 10-year-old rape victim should have the right to an abortion. It does not make it *right or wrong*, and it does not make one view more correct. It simply makes us human beings trying to do our best wherever we find ourselves. There is no use in judging someone's viewpoint harshly because you have not walked in their shoes and had their experiences. Whether you are pro-life or pro-choice, there is legitimacy and truth in your ideas and perceptions, but that does not make them universal.

Pro-life Corner

Religious Viewpoints and the Catholic Church

The entire premise of the pro-life camp is based on religion and the idea of ensoulment. Ensoulment refers to the instant when the fetus attains a soul. Aristotelian metaphysics believed that the soul entered the fetus at 40 days in a male embryo and at 90 days in a female embryo. There was the belief in a quickening that was a sure sign the soul had taken residence. Before the period of quickening or ensoulment, the fetus is not regarded as a person.

What is Quickening?

This simply occurs when a fetus begins to move within the uterus and can be felt by the mother in the form of flutters or bubbles. This quickening usually happens after 16 weeks of pregnancy. According to Roman Catholic theologians, ensoulment is believed to take place at conception when the sperm fertilizes the egg. The Roman Catholic Church believes that at this moment the zygote is a human being. This life cannot be killed, despite the circumstances around conception. The mother could have been raped, she could be comatose or mentally unprepared. The health or well-being of the mother becomes irrelevant at this juncture. It is the life she carries that has more value.

Islamic Views on Abortion

Muslim maulanas believe that abortion is never acceptable but many will consent to it before ensoulment occurs. They place ensoulment at 120 days. They will also allow abortions if the mother's life is in jeopardy, because Islamic law does not regard a fetus as a person. A baby that is born and thriving is considered a person.

The Jewish View

The Jewish tradition varies in its view on ensoulment, but the Talmud regards the fetus as being a part of the mother and a "possible human," but not having its own personhood. They, like the Islamic tradition, believe that the baby that takes its first breath of air is a person. Abortion is allowed especially if it is to save the life of the mother. Jewish tradition is not clear about the other circumstances that could warrant abortions, such as the mother's compromised mental health, observed fetal disabilities, or the mother's lack of resources to support the baby. American Jews support abortion based on actual life versus potential life (Mehta, 2022).

Hinduism and Buddhism

Hinduism takes a varied view from the other dominant world religions with its belief in the wheel of reincarnation, which could support pro-life or pro-choice arguments. It doesn't matter where in the wheel your life ends because you will be born again. Buddhists believe that although it is not the best solution, in some instances it could be the only moral choice. They recognize that life is far too complex to make partisan decisions.

Abortion is Murder!

Sara Sander Lee, Senior Fellow and Director of Life Sciences at the Charlotte Lozier Institute, stated (CNA, 2022):

> Life begins from the moment of con-
> ception when the sperm fertilizes the
> egg because there is the creation of a
> new, totally distinct, integrated organ-
> ism or a
> human being, which is going to be bi-
> ologically distinct from all other life
> forms on this planet.

From a purely scientific perspective, Lee is correct; the moment the zygote forms, the initial genetic blueprint for a unique being is knitted together in the womb. Pro-life advocates and those with
religious bias often use the story of the strenuous
swim of the sperm cell to reach the egg as a race
for life. Out of millions of potential winners, there
is only one that wins the race to fertilize that egg
to produce a potentially unique human with 50%
of the DNA from the sperm cell and 50% from the
egg. An extract from the Catechism of the Catholic
Church says the following about the embryo: "Since
it must be treated from conception as a person, the
embryo must be defended in its integrity, cared for,
and healed, as far as possible, like any other human
being."

Pope Francis, the Pontiff leading the Catholic
Church, has been quite vocal about his anti-abor-

tion sentiment; in recent years he has condemned the act and compared it to Nazi eugenics and murder. Some questions asked of him about abortion elicited the following responses (CNA, 2021):

Abortion is murder!

It is troubling to see how simple and convenient it has become for some to deny the existence of a human life as a solution to problems that can and must be solved
for both the mother and her unborn child. How can an action that ends an innocent and defenseless life in its blossoming stage be therapeutic, civilized or simply human? I ask you: Is it right to 'do away with human life in order to solve a problem? Is it right to hire a hitman in order to solve a problem? One cannot. It is not right to 'do away with a human being, however small, in order to solve a problem. It is like hiring a hitman.

> Abortion is not a theological problem. It is a human problem. It is a medical problem. You kill one person to save another, in the best-case scenario. ... It's against the Hippocratic oaths doctors must take. It is an evil in and of itself.

The Pope is the leader of 1.3 billion believers who regard him as a representative of God on earth. By his pronouncements and responses, he leads 1/8 of the population of the world. A lot of what he says evokes great emotion and anti-abortion sentiment. His comparisons of abortion to Nazi eugenics, hitmen, and murder send a powerful message to communities that their salvation depends on not committing the sin of abortion. It also sends out negative messages to his sees all over the world that the doctors, nurses, and health care workers involved in abortions are hitmen and guilty of gross misconduct. These words can be triggers that set off erratic behavior from fanatics and zealots.

Disposable Culture

We live in a world of mass consumption where everything is disposable and replaceable. It is also a world that thrives on materialism and money, where making a million dollars is far more attractive than raising children. Having babies has become an inconvenience for many young people, especially the millennials who seem to have a totally different philosophy about life and procreation. Many millennials believe the planet is overburdened as it is, and there is no need for more babies to be brought into the world for continued population explosion.

This *disposable* culture has tainted all aspects of our lives—it has reached the sexual habits and practices of young people. Although the church and other religious

institutions preach abstinence until marriage, that is now more the exception than the norm. Advances in medical science, the development of contraceptives, and the women's liberation movement have allowed for sexuality to be more open and acceptable without the threat of pregnancy. We now have the disposable condom, the morning after pill, the contraceptive pill, IUDs, injections, and hormone patches. The world panders to make quick and easy sex available and safer. So what if an accident of nature occurs? You can always dispose of it.

Pro-life enthusiasts believe we have laws that favor the reckless and careless behavior of sexually promiscuous people, giving them options to abort babies when they forget to take the pill, or if the condom bursts. This condonation of poor morals and a gross disregard for human life have created a disposable baby culture. The pro-life camp has the backing of some very influential personalities such as the Pope, Cardinals, Baptist pastors, and campaigners like Alveda King who raise awareness on all forms of social media and promote the banner of pro-life.

Alveda King, the niece of Martin Luther King, Jr., compared abortion to other societal ills (CBC.com, 2022):

> Abortion and racism are both symptoms of a fundamental human error. The error is thinking that when someone stands in the way of our wants, we can justify getting that person out of our lives. Abortion and racism stem from the same poisonous root, selfishness. We create the deception that the other person is less important, less worthy, less human. We are all fully human. When we face this truth, there is no justification for treating those who look different than us as lesser beings. If we simply treat other people the way we'd like to be treated, racism, abortion,

and other forms of inhumanity will be things of the past.

King blames our inherent selfishness about various issues as the root cause of most societal ills, including racism and abortion. She believes human beings have evolved to believe that when we are confronted with a problem or a person who is a problem, our reflex response is to find a way to rid ourselves of the problem. We do not allow ourselves the time to process our thoughts and emotions about the issue. We fail to dig deep within ourselves, to reason and look at how any decision we take will impact the short-term and long-term versions of ourselves. She believes that if more men and women corrected this flaw within themselves, they would be able to deal with issues such as abortion and racism.

King spoke frankly about one of the abortions she had just after the Roe v. Wade verdict in 1973: "Roe v. Wade made it too easy for me to make the fateful and fatal decision to abort my child. The doctor advised that the procedure would hurt no more than 'having a tooth removed.'"

In her television interview, King told viewers about the terrible problems she continued to have with her pelvis as a result of the abortion that caused her to miscarry a fetus she had become pregnant with a short while later. She complained about how having the abortions affected her ability to be emotionally involved with her subsequent children or to bond adequately with them. King has explained how the abortions affected her long afterward because she suffered from eating disorders, depression, nightmares, sexual dysfunctions, and many other issues, as a result of the guilt (CBN.com, 2022). Ms. King has now become a pro-life activist who travels to Washington D.C. to lobby for the rights of unborn children.

Alveda King has raised issues of great concern to many pro-life advocates regarding the lengths human beings have gone to manipulate science to achieve their selfish ends. You don't want a baby, you kill it. This could lead to eugenics, where gene manipulation and "designer babies" could become the norm. It raises the ethical debate about whether doctors have the right to terminate a fetus that is found to be less than perfect and presents with some deformity such as Down's Syndrome or Spina Bifida. If we continue to play God, we are committing genocide by deliberate murder of any being that is less than perfect or unwanted. Then the Pope is correct, we will be no better than the "Angel of Death" Josef Mengele, the Nazi doctor who performed deadly experiments on prisoners in the concentration camps during World War II.

US Supreme Court Justice Clarence Thomas echoes a similar sentiment in trying to ensure that we do not forget what it means to be human (Rosenberg, 2019):

> Abortion is an act rife with the potential for eugenic manipulation. Technological advances have only heightened the eugenic potential for abortion, as abortion can now be used to eliminate children with unwanted characteristics, such as particular sex or disability.

The human race is facing a watershed moment in deciding what makes us human. We have come such a long way from our ancient past. We have evolved from uncivilized and marauding barbarians to uniting in agreement on the Universal Declaration of Human Rights in 1948. The pro-life camp is asking us to uphold the values that make us human and to protect the sanctity of human life.

Pro-life believers assert there is a solution to bringing an end to the murder of the unborn by increasing education and the availability of contraception. Research has been done on the effect of proper sex education on teens in US schools, and they have discovered that those who participated in comprehensive sex education programs seemed to have had sex later on in life than their parents. In a survey conducted in 2019 by the CDC Biannual Youth Risk Behavior Survey, it was found that 38. 4% of American high schoolers reported they have had sex (down from 54% in 1991) and only 27.4% reported they were currently sexually active (37.5% in 1991) (Lehman, 2020). These statistics are used by those supporting the pro-life agenda to indicate that equipping our youngsters with the tools to under-stand their sexuality and to engage in safe sex will reduce the need for abortions over time.

The pro-life agenda is about improving access for young women to the necessary resources such as clinics and contraception. If the pro-life agenda is to abandon abortion, then the political right-wingers will have to change their stance on various health legislation. There will have to be more state expen-ditures on the health of young women, especially minorities. The federal government has to prior-itize young girls and young women and increase their free access to sexual health services and a qual-ity education system.

Pro-choice Corner

Women's Rights

Article One of the Universal Declaration of Human Rights states: "All human beings are born free and equal in dignity and rights. They are endowed with reason and

conscience and should act towards one another in a spirit of brotherhood" (United Nations, 1948).

Apparently, the original statement stated that "All men are born free," but there were many delegates present who were vocal about needing to change this phrase to be

truly inclusive. Delegate Hansa Mehta from India is credited with calling for this phrase to change. The timing for this Declaration was post-WWII and women were still seen as a homemaker, child-bearer, and child-rearer. The old maxim "barefoot and pregnant" was expected of many women, in all cultures around the world.

Women's rights refer to the rights and entitlements for women that gained prominence in the women's rights movements of the 19th century and today. Basic human rights charters differ significantly from women's rights, largely because of women's subordinate roles throughout history.

Some of the issues that dominate the women's rights agenda are

- to vote
- to receive an education
- to be employed
- to earn equal pay as men
- to own property
- to have bodily autonomy
- to be free from violence of any kind
- to be a legal entity (be able to sign a contract)
- to be treated fairly in family courts
- to have reproductive rights
- to occupy leadership positions in organizations and governments

These rights are just a few that could be used to determine whether women in certain countries and cultures enjoy entitled rights. The issue of women's rights takes

center stage, because for millennia, women in different parts of the world enjoyed some rights, but were still dominated by a masculine hegemony. When you

consider the dowry system in India or the lobola system in Africa, women are still regarded as the property of their family or husband. In other cultures, such as Islamic culture, females are deemed as inferior in stature to a man and must accede to the dictates of their parents with regard to marriage and their dressing. Traditionally, in India, young women are not allowed to find their own partners because marriages are arranged.

In Africa, there is evidence that women had more power and equality in pre-colonial times, although their role was to take care of household and agricultural tasks. When colonization began, women became the most oppressed of all the people in Africa, because they were further subjugated by the patriarchy that accompanied colonial rule. Even with liberation from colonial forces, some African countries have failed to restore full rights to women. Many African women still experience gender inequality, shocking levels of poverty, poor education and health access, lack of nutritious food, poor representation in the running of the country, lack of a political voice, limited access to jobs, gender-based violence, child marriages, and genital mutilation.

The same pattern of disadvantage and oppression found in Africa is evident across much of the developing world from South America to the Far East, India, and the Pacific Islands. It's for this reason the United Nations has established the UN Women and Commission on the Status of Women (CSW) which seeks to promote gender equality and empowerment of women around the world. UN Women promotes leadership and political participation, peace, and security; ending violence against women, sustainability issues, disabled rights, rights for young girls, HIV and AIDS focus, humanitarian aid, governance, and planning (2019). Despite all these efforts, women are still one of the most oppressed entities in the world.

Body Autonomy

When you consider women's bodies, they have always been under the control of a patriarchal system. From the time of her birth, she is judged by her sex and her gender. By the design of her anatomy, the vagina can be seen as a receptacle for invasion or plunder from the outside, voluntarily or otherwise. Her body makes her vulnerable to possession by the phallus, or the metaphorical subjugation by the phallic power that surrounds her and threatens to overpower her life, her decisions, and even the control she should enjoy over her own body. The male phallus represents the weapon of authority and domination that can be used for pleasure and punishment. This power dynamic is probably the reason for the state of relations between the sexes today.

If you have watched cartoons or depictions of cavemen, you should be familiar with the woman being dragged by her hair into a cave. This sums up the way women have

been treated by our political and socio-economic systems. She is seen as a lesser other that is child-like and needs to be handled. Laws are supported by males for females with very little consultation about their needs and psychology. If you look at the Constitution of the United States and its signato-ries, it was the work of George Washington, James Madison, and Alexander Hamilton. Conspicuously absent is the signature and input of any woman. Yet women gave birth to these great men and all men who rule this world and make unfair decisions about the welfare of females.

Pro-choice advocates do not accept the rules made for women by a patriarchal system that en-trenches the status quo. A woman's body belongs entirely to herself. She is in charge of her body and is entitled to make decisions about what she chooses to do with it. From a pro-life perspective, abortion is considered an abomination and murder of a person because it goes against the biblical commandment that "thou shalt not kill," but a pro-choice viewpoint would refute this argument and assert that the fetus is not a person yet and abortion is not murder.

Women's Health

Each year, 4.7–13.2% of maternal deaths can be attributed to unsafe abortion. In developed regions, it is estimated that 30 women die for every 100,000 unsafe abortions. In developing regions, that number rises to 220 deaths per 100,000 unsafe abortions. Estimates from 2012 indicate that in developing countries alone, 7 million women per year were treated in hospital facilities for complications of unsafe abortion. (WHO, 2021)

If we review the numbers, it makes sense that where abortions are done in a safe, controlled environment lives of women are saved. By overturning the Roe v. Wade verdict, the Supreme Court is throwing the safety and lives of women out of the window in favor of a fetus that is yet to take its first breath. The laws of the land refer to "living persons"—they were not made for the unborn.

The WHO (2021) believes the following health risks of unsafe abortions support why outlawing safe abortions is a certain disaster:

- It can lead to infections, septicemia, and death.
- It can lead to hemorrhage, which could also be fatal.

- It could result in an incomplete abortion, which could increase infection or result in a disabled baby.

- It could result in uterine perforation if a sharp instrument is used without sufficient knowledge of the female anatomy.

- The introduction of dangerous objects into the genital tract can result in serious damage to the uterus, rectum, and other internal organs.

- It puts women under tremendous stress.

- It could lead to a woman's inability to have any future children.

The United States is choosing to put the lives of young women at risk to satisfy the moral chanting of churchmen and lobbyists. Pro-choice advocates are fighting for women's right to life and dominion over their own bodies.

One of the current debates by pro-choice lobbyists has to do with conditions that may endanger the health of the mother. In some situations, abortion is a medical necessity. In the instance of an ectopic pregnancy, there is no question that it will have to be done to save the life of the woman involved. Ectopic pregnancies occur when the egg is implanted out of the uterine cavity, usually in the fallopian tubes. These types of pregnancies result in 10% of pregnancy-related deaths, and ectopic pregnancies are the number one reason for the death of women in their first trimester (Ries, 2022).

Health care workers are concerned that the adjustment to abortion laws following the recent Roe v. Wade ruling may affect the quality of care that women with ectopic pregnancies will receive. They believe the legislative language may be misunderstood and present barriers to care that could lead to a loss of life. There is a lot of ignorance among lawmakers and state legislators who have been recorded as suggesting the medically impossible—remove the fertilized egg and re-implant in the uterus. Missouri's abortion bill initially banned abortions for ectopic pregnancies, but was later recapitulated because of an outcry from the public.

Early miscarriages require specific drugs for treatment against infections. This refers to drugs such as mifepristone and misoprostol. These drugs block the hormone progesterone. Mifepristone allows for the lining of the uterus to come away, thus ending the viability of the pregnancy. Misoprostol is a prostaglandin that creates contractions in the womb and causes the expulsion of the pregnancy. With revised anti-abortion legislation, some pharmacists may refuse to dispense these drugs for miscarriages or ectopic pregnancies. US Treasury Secretary Janet Yellen stated (Lawder, 2022):

> Eliminating the rights of women to make decisions about when and whether to have children would have very damaging effects on the economy and would set women back decades... In many cases, abortions are of teenage women, particularly low-income and often Black, who aren't in a position to be able to care for children, have unexpected pregnancies, and it deprives them of the ability often to continue their education to later participate in the workforce.

One of the most unfortunate situations research has uncovered is that most unwanted pregnancies occur amongst teenage girls who are Black, Hispanic, or Multi-racial and hail from poorer neighborhoods. These young women generally have limited prospects and access to good medical support. Being able to get an abortion gives these young women the opportunity to complete high school and possibly enter the workforce or pursue further studies. Condemning these previously disadvantaged young women to a life of forced motherhood and poverty is a gross miscarriage of justice. The pro-life camp may argue they had choices and they made the wrong choices, but these girls did not get pregnant by themselves. They are impregnated by the male of the species, yet these girls have to bear the brunt of society's condemnation and ire on their own. It seems that the laws and the church are misogynistic—made by men, run by men, for the benefit of men.

Missouri has proposals to introduce restrictions on allowing its female residents from crossing state lines to acquire abortion pills or medications (Pierson et al, 2022). A bill introduced last year would extend the state's civil and criminal restrictions to providers in states with legalized abortion if the procedure were performed on a Missouri resident. It even applied if a non-resident had sex in the state and it led to conception.

The imposition of these kinds of far-reaching restrictions reeks of autocracy and conservatism bordering on the ridiculous. It does not feel like America any longer. It feels like we have stepped back into our pioneering past when women were brought over as brides in arranged marriages to bear children for their plantation-owner husbands.

The issue of abortion is a heatedly contested one that we can argue about until we are blue in the face but the best way to find answers to these moral dilemmas is to conduct extensive research. Dr. Diana Greene Foster did just this in 2020. She published the results of a 10-year study conducted on women from 21 states titled *The Turnaway Study: Ten Years, A Thousand Women, and the Consequences of Having–or being Denied–an Abortion.* They included women who successfully had an abortion done, and those who were denied abortions.

This study uses the evidence from the lives of 1000 real women to derive a few of the positive outcomes of abortion and how it definitely enhances a women's health and well-being, and that denying women the right to decide for themselves leads to economic and physical distress. The never-ending opposition from anti-abortion groups that are constantly bombarding women with judgments fails to take heed of what is in the best interests of the young woman concerned. It is time for women to decide their own fate and stop being treated as juveniles that need to be 'fathered' and 'disciplined' by a system founded by men who think they know what is morally and legally right for women's bodies (Baker 2020).

The following were some of the findings of this research:

- Those who were denied abortions went on to have the baby and experienced poverty and hardship at least four years after.

- Women who had been denied abortions experienced a lower standard of living and had a shortage of money for food, accommodation, and living expenses for years afterward.

- Women denied abortions had a lower credit score, were more likely to be bankrupt, have an account in arrears, or be evicted.

- These women seem to stay or continue relations with a violent partner.

- They seem to be raising the child alone years later without assistance from the father or family members.

- Children born to mothers denied abortions grow up to have a lowered standard of living.

- Women denied abortion have a problem forming bonds with the baby they were forced to have.

The study showed that the women who were allowed abortions went on to enjoy a much better quality of life, having a family later on, and were in a better position to be

more engaged and financially independent mothers. This study clearly shows the stark differences the pro-choice advocates are speaking about, because bringing an end to abortions will affect the lives of thousands of women and children who will be condemned to a life of poverty and hardship.

Rape and Sexual Assault

The United States is listed as the third highest for rape crimes in the world after South Africa and Sweden. In the United States 83% of females between the ages of 12 and 16 have experienced some form of sexual harassment or rape at a public school (Khan, 2019). Every 107 seconds, someone in the United States is sexually assaulted, with average statistics indicating that in 2019, 406,070 rapes were reported, while in 2020, 298,628 were documented. It's estimated that more than 68% of rape incidences are not reported to the police and that 98% of rapists will not do any prison time (Statista, 2021).

Researchers believe that men rape as a form of aggressive sexual coercion that has a lot to do with having control and power. Most men who rape will do it more than once. In a dissertation titled *The Undetected Rapist,* undertaken for a PhD at Claremont Graduate University by Dr. Smithyman, the researcher was able to gather a great deal of data on rapists who get away with their crimes. He uncovered stories about a man raping his girlfriend, another raping his friend's wife, and a custodian getting away with more than 10 rapes. What surprised Dr. Smithyman was how normal these rapists were—they could be the man next door, your postman, janitor, or best friend (Murphy, 2017).

With the initiation of the #MeToo movement that was kicked off on MySpace by Tarana Burke, a sexual assault victim and survivor, people have been given a voice to publicly unmask perpetrators of sexual violence and rape. It is a move in the right direction for assault victims. But imagine a woman being viciously raped and finding out her trauma was only getting started—that she was pregnant and carrying a reminder of her violation inside her own body. Like in *Rosemary's Baby,* to her, it might as well be the spawn of Satan.

How can any person feel no pity for a woman who has been tortured and forced to submit to the will of a rapist? It should be her right to be taken to the hospital for testing and given the abortion pill and ARVs, if needed. It should be a mandatory practice and the only moral reaction to rape.

After the Dobbs v. Jackson Women's Health Organization decision and the overturning of Roe v. Wade, Ohio placed a ban on any abortions after six weeks gestation with no exceptions for rape or incest. Very soon after this ban, news broke of a

10-year-old who had been raped in Ohio. She was determined to be six weeks and three days pregnant. The child was forced to travel out of state to Indiana in order to get the procedure done. President Biden reacted at the White House when he heard about the case:

> She was forced to have to travel out of the state to Indiana to seek to terminate the pregnancy and maybe save her life. Ten years old—10 years old! Raped, six weeks pregnant, already traumatized, was forced to travel to another state.

After the President's outcry, criticisms were leveled at him for commenting publicly about a story that was not corroborated. Some of the reaction came from Republicans like the Ohio Attorney General Dave Yost and Rep. Jim Jordan, the Wall Street Journal's editorial board. Yost was forced to recant his criticism when a 27-year-old man was arrested for the crime and responded (Bella, 2022):

> My heart aches for the pain suffered by this young child. I am grateful for the diligent work of the Columbus Police Department in securing a confession

and getting a rapist off the street. Justice
must be served and BCI stands ready to
support law enforcement across Ohio in
putting these criminals behind bars.

There needs to be a change in the thinking of
the people who ascend into power with notions
of inherent prejudice and discrimination against
women. The issue of abortion raises many other
cracks in our socio-politico-economic systems that
need to be brought into the light and scrutinized.
The American system is regarded as one of the
oldest evolving democracies from its inception in
1776 but with the recent developments in decisions
taken by the Supreme court and the anti-abortion
sentiment, it is slowly devolving into authoritarian
patriarchy (Soros 2022).

CONTEXTUALIZING ABORTION BEFORE 1973

Perusal of the literature on the history of abortion highlights the fact that abortions existed within some of the most ancient cultures. There is evidence that abortions were done in Indian, Assyrian, Japanese, Māori, Greek, and Roman cultures. A lot of these abortions did not use any instruments and were non-surgical; methods included attempting physical or strenuous activities like climbing, picking up heavy weights, running, jumping, fasting, bloodletting, pouring hot water on the belly, and many other archaic methods based on their limited understanding at the time. They also attempted the use of abortifacients which refer to herbs and concoctions used to induce abortions.

A lot of what has been passed down over the ages comes from the Greco-Roman cultures. There is mention of herbs such as silphium, rue, dill, birthwort, pennyroyal, catnip, hellebore, and a few others. These remedies were carried across the Atlantic by colonial settlers. Early Americans were given recipes for an abortifacient with accurate measurements by none other than Benjamin Franklin. He called the recipe a solution to "the misfortune" of an unwanted pregnancy for "unmarry'd women" (Farrell, 2022). This leads us to believe that abortions existed among early Americans from the time of the founding fathers.

Christianity and Abortion Through History

Aristotle wrote, "The line between lawful and unlawful abortion will be marked by the fact of having sensation and being alive." (Quotefancy, n.d.) Aristotle believed the ensoulment took place around 40 days for males and 90 days for females. St. Augustine believed that the *fetus animatus* (fetus with limbs and arms), when aborted, was called murder, but he took the same stance as Aristotle about abortion in the earlier stages as not being murder before it forms limbs.

In the *Leges Henrici Primi*, written around 1115, around the time of King Henry I, it records that pre-quickening abortion was a misdemeanor, and post-quickening abortion carried a lesser penalty than homicide. Currently, the Roman Catholic Church and Eastern Orthodox Churches oppose abortion on grounds that conception entitles the zygote to personhood and defense as human life. Protestant Churches have varying degrees of tolerance for abortion.

History of Abortion in America

During the 19th century, a lot of changes occurred in the field of medicine including surgery, sanitation, and anesthesia. Up until then, abortion was practiced during the quickening and ensoulment periods, when they were still allowed. In the United States, physicians were the first to talk about criminalizing abortion. They felt the women who were practicing at-home abortions were untrained and unskilled practitioners. There was also the move to question the concept of quickening and to consider conception the beginning of new life.

The English law on abortion was first legislated under sections one and two of the Malicious Shooting or Stabbing Act 1803. "The Bill was proposed by the Lord Chief Justice of England and Wales, Edward Law, 1st Baron Ellenborough to clarify the law relating to abortion and was the first law to explicitly outlaw it" (Doan, 2007). These

English laws were transplanted from English soil and influenced the American drive for similar laws to be introduced. Connecticut was the first state in the United States to outlaw abortion after the quickening period. Soon after, 10 more of the 26 states followed suit. New York enacted penalties for post-quickening abortion as a felony and pre-quickening abortions as a misdemeanor (Buell, 1991). This view began to spread as more people started to realize that when doctors took the Hippocratic Oath, they vowed to protect all human life, and abortion went against this decree. Despite these movements to curtail abortion, there were still abortifacients sold and advertised.

Historians believe that in the 19th century between 15% to 35% of pregnancies ended in abortion. James Mohr who wrote *Abortion in America* in 1978 reveals there were high abortion rates in 19th-century America—"from about one in every thirty live births around 1800 to about one in every five by 1870"—quite in keeping with current trends (Skerry, 1978). In his book, Mohr revealed that in the early days of the 19th century it was mainly unmarried women who were seeking abortions, but this began to change toward the 1850s when abortion became prevalent among middle- and upper-class *married women*. The American Medical Association (AMA) was formed in 1847, and they asserted that physicians were learned scholars with expert knowledge on embryos and the female anatomy, and they should be the authority on abortion. They wanted to take ownership of women's reproductive rights and to control the role of midwives and nurses. The AMA wanted to dictate the terms and conditions when an abortion could be performed. As a result of these changes, a movement against abortion began to gain momentum in the 1880s, led by the medical fraternity. Mohr calls this a physician's crusade, stating (Skerry, 1978):

> The two chief pressures that produced the anti-abortion laws in the first place [were] the short-term interests of regular physicians in the face of an unprecedented crisis in the history of medical practice in the United States and the shift in the sociodemographic role of abortion in America.

Once again, this movement was initiated by male physicians against the practices of unqualified midwives. At that point in America's history, becoming a doctor was seen as a male prerogative and only a few daring, pioneering women dared to challenge the status quo to qualify as medical doctors, such as Elizabeth Blackwell.

Mohr's commentary can be viewed as biased, considering he overlooks the rest of the population that may have driven the spiritual and moral imperative of killing the unborn to protect the lives of women who may have died from abortions performed by inexperienced midwives.

One sector that would have been affected but gained little exposure was women working as slaves on plantations in the United States. These women were bought and paid for, and their offspring were regarded as the property of their masters. Many slaveowners did not condone abortions on their property. It is possible though, that the Black midwives and healers would have had their own abortifacients and folk remedies such as cotton roots, calomel, or turpentine to induce abortions among the slave women.

The Prosperous and the Prostitutes

Around the 19th century, there was increased industrialization and men were starting to travel more on business. This gave rise to what people call the oldest profession in the world—prostitution. It's estimated that by mid-century there were as many as 60,000 prostitutes plying their trade across industrialized America. The women were eager to make good money from transitory businessmen who paid well for quick work, but along with this trade came unwanted pregnancies and the demand for abortions. Abortionists became wealthy from this lucrative trade. Ann Lohman, also known as Madame Restell, became notorious in New York City as an abortionist and "the wickedest woman in New York." She ran an advert in the *New York Sun* on March 18, 1839 (Carlson, 2009):

> TO MARRIED WOMEN.—Is it not but too well known that the families of the married often increase beyond what the happiness of those who give them birth would dictate?... Is it moral for parents to increase their families, regardless of consequences to themselves, or the well-being of their offspring, when a simple, easy, healthy, and certain remedy is within our control? The advertiser,

> feeling the importance of this subject, and estimating the vast benefit resulting to thousands by the adoption of means prescribed by her, has opened an office, where married females can obtain the desired information.

She began receiving clients from about 9 a.m. up to 10 at night. She prescribed pills and potions to help women miscarry; if that didn't work, then she performed surgical procedures at the cost of $20 for poor women and $100 for the wealthier set. Madame Restell was also known to assist with birthing and adoptions. She became well known after she treated a married woman called Maria Purdy. Purdy, who was dying of tuberculosis, confessed to her husband that she had aborted one of their children via Madame Restell. Purdy's husband reported Madame Restell to the police, and she was put on trial and vilified as a "monster in human shape."

Madame Restell published an advertisement in the *New York Herald* in which she offered $100 to anyone who would come forward to prove that she had done any harm

(Abbott, 2012):

> I cannot conceive how men who are husbands, brothers, or fathers can give utterance to an idea so intrinsically base and infamous, that their wives, their sisters or their daughters, want but the opportunity and 'facility' to be vicious, and if they are not so, it is not from an innate principle of virtue, but from fear. What is female virtue, then, a mere thing of circumstance and occasion?

Madame Restell was eventually found not guilty and continued offering her services in Boston and Philadelphia where she called on married women whose deteriorating health made pregnancy dangerous. Restell was also well known for securing "loans" from wealthy clients and not returning the money, knowing full well that they would not want any bad publicity.

Marvin Olasky estimates that about 100,000 prostitute-related abortions took place each year around this time (Abort73.com, 2019).

> Around the 19th century, the women's rights movement was gaining momentum. Physicians began to blame this movement for the increase in abortions

among married women. But this was a matter of perspective, because not many feminists approved of abortions. They were of the opinion that abortion was the last resort of women who were pushed to the brink by callous and thoughtless men.

In the newspaper *The Revolution*, run by Elizabeth Cady Stanton and Susan B. Anthony, they published an article debating that lawmakers should be addressing the proper cause of the increase in abortions rather than calling for the prosecution of those involved. Simply passing an anti-abortion law would:

> ... be only mowing off the top of the noxious weed, while the root remains. ... No matter what the motive, love of ease, or a desire to save from suffering the unborn innocent, the woman is awfully guilty who commits the deed. It will burden her conscience in life, it will burden her soul in death; But oh! thrice guilty is he who drove her to the desperation which impelled her to the crime.

This is the exact sentiment echoed by pro-choice enthusiasts today who recognize that laws and sentencing of women and health care workers is a smokescreen creating a veil around the true perpetrators—the males who are allowed to strut around, ply their sex, and walk away blameless while the woman is vilified.

For almost a century from the 1880s up to 1973, abortions were criminalized. This did not deter women from going the illegal "back alley abortion" route. When the state criminalizes a social movement or activity, it will provoke the people to go underground. This was indicated by abortion, the abolition of alcohol, the LGBT movement, and a host of other movements. The will of the people cannot be underestimated, and the will of a minority should never overshadow that of the individual.

There are stories about the backstreet abortions that would make your skin crawl. Women would be forced to seek out abortionists in desperation from physicians or untrained men who had dodgy setups that were dirty and unsanitary. "The most appalling stories tell of men (some physicians, some not) who performed abortions in filthy settings, under the influence of alcohol, and who demanded sexual favors from their terrified and vulnerable patients" (Joffe, Weitz, & Stacey, 2004). With the criminalization of abortion by the state, only the AMA was tasked with deciding what conditions and situations were allowable for an abortion. However, there was no structure or written document to guide physicians on which abortions to authorize.

Kristin Luker (1984) explains in her book *Abortion and the Politics of Motherhood* that the medical fraternity embraced two divergent paths:

- Strict Constructionists: These were doctors who opposed abortion on moral grounds and sought to administer the most stringent interpretation of laws governing

  abortion.

- Broad Constructionists: These used a more broad and discretionary interpretation of the abortion laws.

It was difficult for doctors working within this contradictory framework to make sense of what constituted a proper legal abortion and what bordered the illegal. In the 20th century, before 1973, more of the patients who were asking for abortions did not fit the criteria for a legal abortion because their lives were not in danger. Doctors were in a quandary as to what to do. There were doctors who were more sympathetic, and those who were morally incensed. The strict constructionist doctors were sometimes exposed to the terrible ravages of back alley abortions or women trying to abort their own babies. They encountered women who were seriously injured with infections and septicemia. They could not avoid the harsh realities of turning away a desperate woman and having them return as patients whose lives were hanging in the balance because of their stringent decisions about abortion. So, many of them capitulated and allowed some of the abortions to be performed, even though it went against their strict moral codes.

Before Roe 1973, it is reported that hospitals had to establish special wards to care for women with botched abortions. These wards were mockingly referred to as "septic tanks" by the doctors and nurses. This referred to the sepsis that would occur in the woman's bloodstream due to illegal abortions. Conservatively, it is estimated that the death of women as a result of illegal abortions was around 5,000 in the years before the Roe verdict.

Criminalizing Abortion

The first abortion laws made their way into written law in the early part of the 19th century where most of it was focused on patent medicines or abortifacients, and abortions that were not allowed after the quickening. The first codified law was laid down in 1821 in Connecticut which declared that any person who provided or took poison or other noxious and destructive substance with the intention of causing abortion or miscarriage would be punished. By the mid-1800s, physicians touted the view that only licensed doctors should be allowed to control women's reproductive issues and not female midwives.

Gynecologist Horatio Storer was a Harvard-educated obstetrician who led the medical establishment in the US to take a stance against abortions. In 1857, after being with the American Medical Association (AMA) for a year, he began his crusade of criminalizing abortion. He argued that abortion was an immoral choice and was responsible for "derangement" in women. He lobbied for the AMA to view abortion as a crime. Storer, who was seen as the father of gynecology, was also seen as a single warrior who led the AMA to call for stringent statutes and limitations on abortion. He pushed for a Committee on Criminal Abortion to be formed. Storer became the Chairman of the Committee and was tasked to prepare a report.

In 1865, Storer wrote a paper called *The Origins of Insanity in Women*, which he delivered to the AMA congress. In this paper, he suggested the introduction of "ovariectomies," arguing that for women who "have become habitually thievish, profane, or obscene, despondent or self-indulgent, shrewish or fatuous," the best solution is to "remove the cause": a woman's reproductive organs (Aron, 2017). Storer used a woman's need for an abortion as grounds to try to end her ability to ever conceive a child as punishment for the act. He had a problem with abortions being allowed before quickening, and challenged his fellow doctors to see the fetus as a "possible man," a person, and to regard abortion as a crime against a living "person." Storer's report was unanimously accepted and adopted in 1859 and remained its official policy until 1967. His stranglehold on the way abortion laws were enacted and maintained lasted for 114 years until Roe v. Wade in 1973.

Storer comes across as a controlling, sexist misogynist who regarded women who had abortions as loose women who needed to be taught their role in society. He said the following in an essay he wrote for the AMA titled *Why Not? A Book for Every Woman*, for which he was rewarded with a prize:

> If these wretched women, these married, lawful mothers, ay, and these Christian husbands, are thus murdering their children by thousands through ignorance, they must be taught the truth;

> but if, as there is reason to believe is
> too often the case, they have been influ-
> enced to do so by fashion, the extrava-
> gance of living, or lust, no language of
> condemnation can be too strong.

There were many factors that prompted this radical stance—some blame it on the greater influx of
immigrants, others on urban growth or the end of
slavery.

Storer and his colleagues did not approve of
abortions for another reason: he argued that white
women needed to have more babies and to stop
having abortions because the white race needed
to keep their numbers up to still exercise control.
Abortion was regarded as a social evil by the pro-life
proponents and they expressed moral indignation
at the practice. During the 18th and 19th centuries
there was an influx of immigrants from different
parts of the world, which led to increased urbaniza-
tion. Around the same time slavery came to an end
and fear grew amongst the conservative white population that they would lose their control as a majority. The sentiment that they needed to have more
children to continue their dominance grew. This
is the reason for Storer arguing that white women,

especially, had to abstain from procuring abortions to continue the "future destiny of the nation."

The criminalization of abortion continued through the 1860s driven by political players and the AMA. In 1873, Anthony Comstock influenced the United States Congress to pass the Comstock Law, which made the delivery of mail that contained "obscene, lewd or lascivious" material illegal. It also forbade the production, importation, and distribution of any abortion-related material, and prevention of venereal diseases as an obscenity that could be prosecuted. The Comstock Law was passed by 24 out of 37 states (Bennett, 1878).

By 1900, abortion became a felony in every state in the America, although some states still allowed abortions in extreme instances when the life of the mother was at risk, in the case of rape, or when there was incest.

Margaret Sanger was the fiercest advocate of women's reproductive rights. She blamed her mother's death and poverty on her having to birth 11 children and suffer seven miscarriages. She worked as a nurse and was a witness to the botched abortions and death of women as a result. Sanger opened up the first birth control clinic in the United States in 1916. She was arrested for contravention of the Comstock Law and spent a month in jail. The court ruled that women could be given birth control for medical purposes. As a result, she founded the American Birth Control League, which is known today as Planned Parenthood. Sanger had the idea of a pill that could be taken to stop pregnancy. She collaborated with Gregory Pincus and International Harvester in the 1950s to develop the first oral contraceptive pill called Enovid which got FDA approval in 1960.

During the late 1960s, a sexual revolution took place in the United States. There was a liberalization of values and attitudes. With the introduction of the pill, women became more inclined to explore their sexuality without the worry of pregnancy. However, there was a problem with unmarried women or single women accessing the pill through the NHS or clinics of the Family Planning Association. Unwanted pregnancies became a huge problem in the 1960s. In 1960, 27% of births of newly married women were less than eight months because single women were forced to marry, or would be sent to a home to have the baby or give it up for adoption. Adoptions of infants rose from 9,214 in 1961 to 12,308 in 1966 (Paintin, 1998).

Here are some of the pre-Roe cases that challenged perceptions:

- Sherri Chessen (1962): She took some sleeping pills that her husband purchased overseas and had no idea they contained thalidomide, which could affect the fetus. Chessen was pregnant with her fifth child when she was informed that her unborn baby had deformities. Her doctor suggested a therapeutic abortion which was allowed in Arizona at the time. Chessen spoke to a newspaper to publicize the danger of thalidomide and requested to remain anonymous, but unfortunately, her identity was revealed, and there were backlash and death threats from anti-abortion activists. Chessen had to fly to Sweden to acquire an abortion amid controversy back in the United States.

- Gerri Santoro (1964): She lived in Connecticut and died after a botched abortion. Her photograph became a symbol of the pro-choice movement.

- The "Jane" Group: A group of women's rights activists in Chicago created an anonymous network to assist women who needed abortions to acquire them in a safe space. They would post messages and a number that desperate women could call. They would be given explicit instructions on how the group's floating clinic would assist them to get the help they needed.

- Tileston v. Ullman, 318 U.S. 44 (1943): This case was against a physician who was accused of giving three patients professional guidance on the use of contraceptives to avoid pregnancy which could have affected the health of the mother.

- Poe v. Ullman, 367 U.S. 497 (1961): This case challenged a Connecticut law that banned the use of contraceptives and banned doctors from prescribing them.

- Griswold vs. Connecticut (1965): Estelle Griswold and Dr. Buxton were arrested after they opened up a clinic in 1961 to administer birth control advice to women. They were charged $100 each. In 1965, the Supreme Court delivered a 7-2 decision in favor of Griswold to allow contraceptives to be administered to married couples.

- Eisenstadt v. Baird, 405 U.S. 438 (1972): This Supreme Court decision allowed unmarried couples to access contraception, effectively legalizing pre-marital sex.

Abortion Data

Although we do not have valid statistics from the 16th century to the 19th century, we do know that abortion was firmly rooted as a part of life for many of the women who lived in the United States. The Native Americans, slaves, and the colonial descendants all had their own abortifacients and emmenagogic herbs (herbs that stimulate menstruation and the shedding of the uterine lining). This meant that women controlled their own bodies, and midwives who learned this tradition from the elders continued to offer the services.

Rachel Gold (2004) comments on the data and estimates that one could extrapolate by looking at the statistics provided by the AMA, hospitals, and other agencies. The following data were estimates of deaths of women from illegal abortions:

- In the 1930s 2,700 women died—1/5 of all maternal deaths in that year.
- In the 1940s the death toll was 1,700.
- In the 1950s the death toll declined to 300.
- By 1965, the death toll was under 200.

The above statistics made clear that as the decades passed, there was a drastic decrease in the death toll. This could be attributed to the increase in knowledge about human anatomy, proper hygiene and sanitation, availability of antibiotics, availability of contraception, and hospital care. Despite the slowdown in the death rate, illegal abortions continued their upward spiral.

- During the 1950s and 1960s, estimates are between 200,000 and 1.2 million per annum.
- A study from North Carolina in 1967 indicated that 829,000 illegal abortions were performed.

- A study of low-income women in New York in the 1960s showed that one in ten women had tried to have an illegal abortion. Four out of ten indicated that a friend, relative, or acquaintance had tried to get an illegal abortion. Eight out of ten women indicated they tried to induce an abortion on their own. Only two percent indicated they had any assistance from a doctor.

- In 1962, 1,600 women were admitted to Harlem Hospital Center in New York with complications due to botched or incomplete abortions.

- In 1968, 701 women were admitted to the University of Southern California Los Angeles County Medical Center with sepsis from abortions.

Who Are These Women Who Choose to Have Abortions?

Many studies across the United States have discovered that the mortality rate from illegal abortions is far higher among women of color than white women. In New York, during the 1960s only one in four white women would die from abortion-related complications, whereas this figure was as high as one in two for Hispanic or Black women. It is apparent this has more to do with poverty and a lack of capital, support, or resources. Minority women comprise the group most affected by the imposition of anti-abortion laws. The CDC estimated that in 1972, 130,000 minority women had an illegal or self-induced abortion and 39 of these women died. They also found that from 1972 to 1974, the abortion mortality rate of minorities was 12 times higher than that of white women (Gold, 2004).

Between 1967 and 1973, women had to appeal for permission to get an abortion under certain circumstances:

- If she could prove that the pregnancy threatened her life.

- If she was physically or mentally incapable of carrying a pregnancy to full term.

- If the pregnancy was a result of rape or incest.

In many states, the woman seeking an abortion would have had to follow a long, arduous process including applications to a hospital committee. The hospital committee would have to be under advisement of state law. The woman involved would also be requested to be checked by physicians other than her own and would undergo various tests and procedures. There could have been requests for a psychiatrist to examine the woman to deem her mental state, especially if it was a case of rape, incest, or mental issues. If it was a case of rape, reports and testimony by a police officer may have been requested. The women who managed to go through the process had to have money and be under the care of a committed, private physician. In a study on 2,775 therapeutic abortions that were undertaken between 1951 and 1962 at New York's private non-profit hospitals, 88% were under the care of a private physician.

Gold states, "The abortion to the live-birth ratio for white women was five times that of nonwhite women, and 26 times that of Puerto Rican women" (2004). This tells us that the socioeconomic standing of these women played a major role in their ability to acquire an abortion.

Another option that the wealthier women had was the option of traveling out of the country to get an abortion. In 1967, England legalized abortions and women from outside the country were able to travel to England to procure an abortion if they could get authorization that was signed by two physicians for the procedure to be done. More than 600 American women traveled to England to have the procedure done by the end of 1969. In 1970, tour operators were offering package deals for women to travel overseas to obtain abortions. In the same year, Hawaii, Washington, New York, and Alaska repealed some of their anti-abortion laws to allow abortions, especially if the woman had been resident in the state for 30 days.

In 1972, over 100,000 women crossed state lines to get a legal abortion in New York. The Guttmacher Institute suggests that about 50,000 women traveled more than 500 miles to get an abortion in New York, as it was the only state that did not require the 30-day residence stipulation. Young women arrived from as far as Nevada, Idaho, and Arizona. Women who arrived from out of state were not eligible for Medicaid at the state hospitals, so these women had to have the cash to pay for travel, accommodation, and hospital expenses. Data shows that 8 out of 10 out-of-state women seeking abortions were white, while 7 out of 10 in-state residents were non-white.

Evidence indicates that just 10% of women living in New York sought an abortion after the 12th week of gestation, while 23% of out-of-state women had abortions after the 12th week of gestation (Gold, 2004).

In assessing the body of research on abortions before 1973, it is evident that wealth, class, and race were not factors that stopped a woman from seeking an abortion. Young women, married women, single women, prostitutes, mentally ill women, abused women, and women from all walks of life felt compelled at some point in their lives to seek out assistance to have an abortion.

Reagan (2008) quotes the words of a physician in 1911:

> Those who apply for abortions are from every walk of life, from the factory girl to the millionaire's daughter; from the laborer's wife to that of the banker, no class, no sect seems to be above . . . the destruction of the fetus.

There is no fundamental difference between a wealthy woman and a poor woman—they have the same body and probability of conceiving a baby. They also have their own thoughts and beliefs, and their own circumstances and personal reasons for not wanting to have a baby. Knowledge about abortion techniques and traditional methods of dealing with illnesses was usually passed down by the older ladies in society. They knew of these traditional methods because abortion was a part of the experience of women for centuries. The various methods had been tried and tested.

As knowledge of women's anatomy improved with strides made in science and gynecology, women would share their knowledge and discoveries with each other. Older ladies shared the traditional techniques known to them; younger women shared the more modern and scientific information.

Reagan (2008) asserts that this was displayed during the early 20th century when a physician cautioned a young married woman of the danger of sepsis, and she responded, "My friend told me to boil my catheter before using it."

Research by Barbara Lesley Brookes (2013), in her book *Abortion in England, 1900-1967*, found that English women at the turn of the 20th century helped each other to induce abortions. She speaks about a woman called Annie K. who had induced three pregnancies and assisted others to do the same.

Mothers and grandmothers helped each other in their time of need. Women generally helped their sisters, daughters, nieces, and friends find someone who could assist with an abortion. Reagan (2008) says, "The willingness of female relatives to obtain abortions for their kin cut across class, from the wealthiest to the poorest families."

Abortions became a necessity in middle-class conservative families during the late 19th century. If their unmarried daughters became pregnant, their mothers would source an abortionist so that the daughter concerned would have better prospects for marriage and to deal with the shame.

Part of the problem was that women did not have a proper understanding of the science behind conception and their monthly cycle. According to census data, the average American woman gave birth to seven or eight children in 1800, but this number dropped to about four children in 1900. Pregnancy and childbirth can take their toll on a woman's physical and mental health, especially during the previous centuries when women were expected to cook, clean, and care for the children and had very little stimulation outside the home.

Illegal Abortions Before 1973

In desperation, women would seek out ways to stop being pregnant and many of them would have tried anything to get rid of the fetus growing inside them. Grimes (2015) explains the many ways that back alley abortions are used to abort babies.

Oral Treatments

- turpentine
- bleach
- detergents
- herbal teas
- vegetable teas

- quinine
- chloroquine (malaria medication)
- over-the-counter drugs, illegally procured drugs like oxytocin, prostaglandins, ergot alkaloids

Vaginal and Uterine Treatments

- potassium permanganate inserted in the vagina causing chemical burns
- pumping toxic mixtures such as chili peppers
- chemicals like Lysol and plant poison could result in toxic shock and death
- soap and turpentine squirted into the uterus causing kidney failure and death
- strange objects inserted into the uterus such as knitting needles, a large feather, bicycle spoke, ballpoint pens, chicken bone, rubber catheter, wire clothes hangers

Dr. Daniel Mishell, Jr. of Los Angeles remembers conditions before Roe (Grimes, 2015):

> They jabbed into their uteruses with knitting needles and coat hangers, which Mishell sometimes found still inside them. They are stuck in bicycle pump nozzles, sometimes sending a fatal burst of air to the heart. They'd

try to insert chemicals—drain cleaner, fertilizer, radiator-flush—and miss the cervix, corrode an artery and bleed to death. Mishell once put a catheter into a woman's bladder and got a tablespoon of motor oil. I'm telling you, it was really an awful situation. It touched me because I'd see young, [otherwise] healthy women in their 20s die from the consequences of an infected nonsterile abortion. Women would do anything to get rid of unwanted pregnancies. They'd risk their lives. It was a different world, I'll tell you.

This is a shocking reality that many lawmakers and men in power fail to grasp. When the legal route is blocked, women will take the illegal path and expose themselves to the most denigrating and dangerous procedures that could maim, burn, puncture, kill, and injure. These women whom the churches and politicians condemn are your mothers, sisters, daughters, friends, girlfriends, mistresses, and lovers. They are real people who deserve the right to decide what's best for their own bodies. It's unfair for anyone to force women into a corner where they could die.

Legal Action Taken Against Transgressors

In 20 states, there were stringent anti-abortion laws and statutes that were enacted. In the *Brief for Appellant-Statutes Involved*, the following laws imposed in Texas during the 1960s are described:

Punishment For Procuring an Abortion

Article 1191 set forth a punishment of two to five years' imprisonment for "any person" who would "procure an abortion" for a pregnant woman by

- "designedly administered... any drug or medicine"

- "knowingly procure, to be administered... any drug or medicine"

- using "towards her any violence or means whatever externally or internally applied"

- the penalty would double "if it be done without her consent"

Accomplice Liability

Article 1192 set forth accomplice liability for any person who "furnishes the means for procuring an abortion knowing the purpose intended."

Punishment for Attempting to Procure an Abortion

Article 1193 sets forth a fine of $100-$1,000 for a person who engages in means "calculated to produce" an abortion but that fails to do so.

Death of the Mother is Murder

Article 1194 set forth that, "if the death of the mother is occasioned" by abortion or attempted abortion, "it is murder."

Exception: Medical Advice Intended to Save the Mother's Life

Article 1196 included an exception for an abortion "procured or attempted by medical advice for the purpose of saving the life of the mother."

Massachusetts was the first state that instituted a law to make abortion a criminal offense in the 1800s. By the early part of the 20th century, almost every state had criminalized abortion. By the early '60s, all types of abortions were forbidden in Pennsylvania while 44 states agreed to abortions only when the mother's life was at risk. Alabama, Colorado, New Mexico, Massachusetts, and the District of Columbia sanctioned abortion if the life or physical health of the woman was at risk; Mississippi approved abortions in case of rape, or if the life of the mother was threatened.

Although the threat of legal action was bandied about for aiding, abetting, advising, and assisting a woman to get an abortion, it was rare for women to actually be convicted. Women would be brought in for questioning if accused of trying to procure an abortion; they would undergo strict interrogations to ascertain the individuals responsible for actually carrying out the abortion. Shirley Wheeler was one of the rare women who was prosecuted in 1971. Medical staff at a Florida hospital contacted law enforcement and reported that she had an illegal abortion. She was charged with manslaughter and received two-year probation. Wheeler received a great deal of support from various quarters such as the Playboy Foundation and the Boston Women's Abortion Coalition. Her conviction was eventually overturned by the Supreme Court of Florida (Lane, 2022).

ROE V. WADE

In the preceding chapters, there was an exploration of abortion in the 19th century up to 1970. Before we begin to understand the Roe v. Wade case in 1973, let us look at a quick summary of the abortion laws and statutes before and after Roe (Eastside Gynecology, 2019):

- 1821: Anti-abortion law passed in Connecticut, this was the first restrictive abortion law that made it illegal for a woman who was with child to take in any oral substance or herbal teas that could result in an abortion. This referred to abortifacients such as pennyroyal and other drugs.

- 1860: Twenty states enforced laws against abortion.

- 1873: The Comstock Law criminalized contraception and abortion; it was allowed in extreme circumstances when recommended by a qualified physician.

- 1890: More laws restricting abortion, except in extraordinary cases, were instituted.

- 1896: The Chicago Health Department imposed stringent limitations on the role and functions of midwives. There was a move to limit midwives' access to abortion

instruments to conduct any procedures. There was a smear campaign against abortionists and midwives.

- 1965: *Griswold v. Connecticut* ruled in favor of a woman's privacy and access to contraception.

- 1966: The National Conference of Catholic Bishops assigned Monsignor James T. McHugh to document abortion reform laws across the different states. As a result, many anti-abortion groups began forming in 1967.

- 1967: Colorado relaxed its abortion laws.

- 1968: Monsignor McHugh was a part of a group that formed the National Right to Life Committee.

- 1969: NARAL Pro-Choice America opposed abortion restrictions.

- 1970-74: More states relaxed their abortion laws (including Alaska, Hawaii, New York, and Washington).

- 1971: *USA v. Vuitch* in Washington D.C. allowed abortion to protect the life of the mother.

- 1972: *Eisenstadt v. Baird* resulted in married couples having the right to information involving contraception.

- 1972: Thirteen states allowed abortion when a woman's health was at risk.

- 1972: By the end of the year, there were states where abortion was illegal and 20 states where it was legal. A woman had to travel to states where abortions were legal to get an abortion.

- 1973: Elected and voluntary abortions remained illegal until the Roe v. Wade case when it was ruled that women had the right to privacy, which included their decision to terminate.

- 1976: The *Hyde Amendment* passed, preventing the funding of abortion through Medicaid.

- 2000: *Stenberg v. Carhart* ruled against the ban on partial-birth abortions by Nebraska law. The ruling on this case by the Supreme Court eliminated 29 other statewide bans.

- 2003: After it was passed by Congress, President Bush signed into law a federal ban on all abortion procedures, this was immediately struck down by the National Abortion Federation in court.

The trend that is observed over the last few centuries is that abortion of fetuses before the quickening was an acceptable act managed by the older and more experienced women in society. This was challenged as people became more educated, especially by the ruling class dominated by males. The restrictions that followed were brought forward by physicians who wanted to control the fertility of women. We find that as there was a swing toward criminalizing abortion across America, there was an equal and opposite tension from other quarters such as the pro-choice movement, the more liberal doctors, and some feminist groups.

During the 1960s, there were cases like *Griswold v. Connecticut*, and *Eisenstadt v. Baird* that saw a swing toward the left and a slight relaxation on the use of contraceptives for married and single women, which set the stage for the Roe v. Wade case in 1973. To truly understand this verdict, we have to contextualize the time, dominant culture, status of women, education, and socio-political situation.

The most reliable way to compare the difference is to study the available statistics. Shin, Siegel, and Mellnik (2022) compared the statistics from 1970 to 2020, and it allows us to get a clear perspective on how much has changed for women since the 1970s. It also allows us to infer how difficult life was for women at that time.

- In 1970, 81% of women aged 24 to 34 were married. In 2020, 43% of women aged 24 to 34 were married. This is a clear indication of the roles of women in 1970, which was mainly to be married early and to be wife, mother, and homemaker. Fifty years later, women are busy with their own careers and postpone marriage and children.

- In 1970, 21% of women were child-free. In 2020, 52% of women were child-free. There are a number of reasons why women delay having children until their thirties. Some of these reasons include education and the prospect of a career that cannot be interrupted by pregnancy. Women tend to be side-lined for upward mobility in a company if they are absent on accouchement leave. There has been a shift in culture with a greater acceptance of women being independent and autonomous. The most important factor is the strides made in medical technology such as in-vitro fertilization, freezing of eggs, egg donors, surrogacy, and hormone replacement therapy. Women now have options, as in the case of 65-year-old Romanian Adriana Iliescu, who gave birth via egg donor because she did not have these options 30 years ago.

- In 1970, 11% of women aged 25 to 44 had a college degree. In 2020, 42% of women aged 25 to 44 had a college degree. Education is by far the

single most important reason for the changes that
have affected women and the decisions around their
physical and productive health. Educating a woman
is educating a nation. In the past, women did not
question their role as homemakers and mothers.
Today, women can reason that having too many
children reduces the quality of life of their family
if they are not earning enough to maintain their
dependents. Women make up a greater percentage
of people graduating from university in most countries of the world. Education empowers women to
become equal partners in the home, earn money
and contribute to the home and children. Women
understand that they can delay marriage and children to pursue a career.

• In 1970, 55% of women aged 15 to 44 did not
have a paid job or were looking for one. In 2020,
27% of women aged 15 to 44 did not have a paid job
or were looking for one. In 1970, it was not a top
priority for women to have a paid job because the
roles of women were different. Women were more
focused on their traditional roles and duties such
as procuring a good marriage, setting up a home,
and having children. Women were taken care of by
their fathers or husbands. That is certainly not the
case in 2020, when women are expected to stand
on their own two feet and take equal responsibility

in running a home. Women in the 21st century are often single mothers and sole breadwinners.

- In 1970, 17% of women aged 16 to 44 held jobs in management. In 2020, 45% of women aged 16 to 44 held jobs in management. In 1970, women were only beginning to be given credit for their work and education. In the present, the sky's the limit for women who compete as equals in the workplace with men in the United States. The same is not true for other countries. In America, there have been several changes and amendments to the law, especially regarding sexual discrimination in the workplace. One such ruling was in the Pittsburgh Press Co. v. Pittsburgh Commission on Human Relations in 1973 when gender-specific job adverts were contested.

- In 1970, 8% of women of child-bearing age earned more than their spouses. In 2020, 27% of women of child-bearing age earned more than their spouses. This statistic is indicative of what the economy looked like in the '70s. It's evident that men of that period were often paid far more than women, and occupied senior and

management positions in most cases. This trend has changed in the last five decades as the role of women changed.

Understanding the United States Supreme Court

The United States Supreme Court is regarded as the highest tribunal and usually hears cases that have already gone through courts in their respective states, either the highest court in a state, or the United States Court of Appeals. Article III of the Constitution states: "The judicial Power of the United States, shall be vested in one supreme Court, and in such inferior Courts as the Congress may from time to time ordain and establish."

The Supreme Court was first set up in 1789 and consists of a Chief Justice and nine Associate Justices. The Supreme Court receives approximately 8,000 petitions per term, but will only hear 80 or so. A term runs from October to the end of June. Each party gets 20 minutes of argument time; there are no juries or witnesses but the Supreme Court has receipt of all the records of the lower courts (Bahn, 2022).

Was There Political Manipulation in the Roe v. Wade Hearing?

There were nine judges who sat for the Roe v. Wade hearing in 1973. Seven judges ruled that abortion was allowed by the United States Constitution.

They were
- Warren E. Burger (Chief Justice)
- William O. Douglas
- William J. Brennan, Jr.
- Potter Stewart
- Thurgood Marshall
- Lewis F. Powell, Jr.
- Harry Blackmun

Justice Blackmun was responsible for the writing up of this historic decision that went on to change the entire legal landscape for women and choices for their bodies. Although Justice Blackmun is given credit for the majority of the document, there were valuable contributions made by Associate Justices Burger, Douglas, and Stewart (Garrett, 2022).

The Associate Justices who did not agree with the verdict were Byron White and William Rehnquist.

There was a belief that this decision was taken because of the appointments of liberal Justices appointed by the Democrats. The shocking truth is that four of the Justices were nominated by republican President Nixon and two other Justices were also

Republicans nominated by other presidents, while only three were nominated by the Democrats.

Chief Justice Burger

Burger was personally nominated by Nixon himself. He was confirmed on June 9, 1969. Burger was one of the Justices who agreed that abortion should be a right for women. He would be the one to write the US v. Nixon decision that eventually led to the resignation of the President after the Watergate scandal. He remained a Republican throughout his life and was conservative in many of his beliefs.

Harry Blackmun

Justice Blackmun was nominated by President Nixon and was a lifelong Republican. He received his nomination in 1970. It is believed that Blackmun and Burger were initially of the same ideological views at the beginning, but Blackmun drifted into a more liberal stance than Burger over time.

William J. Brennan Jr.

Brennan was nominated by President Eisenhower in 1958. He was involved in the McCarthy hearings and offended Senator Joseph McCarthy by referring to him as a witch hunter. He is considered a liberal judge.

William O. Douglas

Douglas was nominated by President Roosevelt in 1939. He was one of the longest-serving judges. People consider him one of the more liberal Justices.

Thurgood Marshall

Marshall was the first Black Democrat Justice to be nominated to the Supreme Court. He was nominated by President Lyndon B. Johnson, a Democrat, in 1967. Marshall is considered one of the more progressive Justices to serve in the Supreme Court. When current Vice President Kamala Harris, the first woman and the first person of African-American and Asian descent was elected as Vice President, she asked to be sworn in on a Bible that had belonged to Marshall.

Lewis F. Powell Jr.

Powell was nominated by President Nixon, but was a Democrat. Powell was regarded as a powerful swing voter on the court.

William H. Rehnquist

Rehnquist was the fourth Justice to be nominated by President Nixon and was probably the most conservative Republican. He was appointed as Chief Justice by President Reagan in 1986.

Potter Stewart

Stewart was nominated to the Supreme Court in 1958 by Dwight D. Eisenhower. Stewart was considered a judicial moderate who took a stronger line on criminal matters, but was more of a liberal on personal and civil issues.

Byron White

White was nominated by John F. Kennedy. He was a Democrat and a Catholic, and his religious beliefs seemed to have influenced his opposition in the Roe v. Wade case.

When discussions first began, there were seven Justices who had already been appointed to the Court. President Nixon appointed two new Justices in 1971, Powell and Rehnquist. Chief Justice Warren Burger, who was also appointed by Nixon, was responsible for insisting on including the two new appointees Powell and Rehnquist in fresh discussions on the issue. Justice Brennan was convinced that the addition of more Nixon appointees left little chance for a decision that would favor a positive verdict for Jane Roe.

An assessment of the leanings of the Justices indicates that there was no posturing or political maneuvering that took place for the Roe v. Wade verdict. In fact, the outcome was a surprising victory because there seemed to be more conservative Justices on the bench. It was a decision that was taken by a fair spread of beliefs and leanings, with an almost even distribution of liberal and conservative views. For once, there was an honest, true confrontation of women's issues with Roe v. Wade, and it was representative of millions of women in the country. After many centuries of struggle, a decision was made for the benefit of women in the United States.

Events Leading Up to Roe v. Wade 1973

Texas was one of the states that instituted anti-abortion legislation during the 1960s and prohibited any type of abortion being performed within state lines, except in cases where the mother's life was in jeopardy. Into this fray appears Jane Roe (Norma McCorvey) who wanted the right to abort in 1969. At this time, Norma McCorvey's identity was still a secret, and only the courts knew some of her histories.

To understand Jane Roe (or Norma McCorvey), you had to know her as a whole person and not just as a woman who wanted a termination. She had a troubled adolescence punctuated with rebelliousness. She spent her teens in a Catholic boarding school and was sent to a reform school for troubled teens. She dropped out of school in ninth grade. Research indicates that she was beaten up by her mother who disagreed with her "wild" behavior and sexual promiscuity with both men and women (Langer, 2017). Norma married Elwood McCorvey when she was just a teen, but the marriage did not last long. She had a daughter out of this marriage who was raised by her mother.

When Roe became pregnant with her second child, she was not married and had the baby adopted. She then became pregnant with her third child in 1969. She had no chance of traveling out of state to seek a termination, nor did she have the capital to travel overseas. She had two choices—have the baby and give it up for adoption, or seek permission to have the fetus legally terminated. McCorvey was an impoverished young woman from the other side of the tracks. She had no intention of becoming

the voice and symbol for other women in America who were poor, pregnant, and with no prospects. She was just a woman who could not afford to support a child, but was being forced to do so by the law of her state.

She was encouraged by an adoption lawyer to speak to Linda Coffee. Linda Coffee and Sara Weddington were recent law graduates looking for someone who could help them challenge the constitutionality of abortion laws in the Supreme Court.

According to Weddington, many women were forced to leave the state or leave the country to secure an abortion. At the time, Weddington had not disclosed that she had been personally affected by the unfair abortion laws when she became pregnant in 1967 during her third year in law school. She was forced to travel to Mexico to get an illegal abortion. She only disclosed this fact in 1992 (Green, 2022). This case was very close to her heart because she had empathy for the plight of Jane Roe who did not have the advantages that she had. Roe did not have the option or the means to seek a termination across state lines.

The case was filed in 1970 by Weddington and Coffee on behalf of McCorvey and all other women "who were or might become pregnant and want to consider all options," against Henry Wade, the District Attorney of Dallas County (Editors, 2022).

The Supreme Court Justices ruled against a Texas statute that forbade abortion except when it threatened the life of the mother. They declared it unconstitutional.

The Supreme Court declared that forbidding abortion undermined the woman's right to privacy. The verdict stated that withholding abortion violated the woman's right to choose what was best for her own person. They ruled that abortions would be legal until the point of viability, which would be determined by the attending doctor conducting the abortion. It also declared that after viability, a doctor could also determine suitability for abortion if it placed the mother's life in danger or was not in the best interests of the mother's psychological health.

One of the core issues in the Roe v. Wade case was when personhood begins. This has been an ongoing debate throughout the centuries. The Roman Catholic church insists it occurs at conception, other religions accept that it is after the quickening, and some say that it occurs only once the baby is born. The Court could not make a decision in this regard and stated (1994):

> We need not resolve the difficult question of when life begins. When those trained in the respective disciplines of medicine, philosophy, and theology are unable to arrive at any consensus, the judiciary, at this point in the development of man's knowledge, is not in a position to speculate as to the answer... the unborn have never been recognized... as persons in the whole sense.

The Justices decided that if neither the churches and other religions, nor science or philosophers could conclude on when life begins, they could not pretend to be any wiser. They made the decision that the 14th Amendment afforded women the right to privacy, and that only she could decide within the legal framework provided by the government what she could do with her pregnancy until the point of viability.

In the discussion that took place among the Justices, it was decided to approach the pregnancy in trimesters. In their discussions, Justice Blackmun, in the initial agreement with the other Justices, felt that in the first trimester the fetus was not viable and termination would be acceptable. After receiving a note from Justice Powell stating he was of the opinion there should be an extension of the period that should be considered for abortion, Justice Blackmun thought that Powell had a fair argument and conceded that the period be extended. He said, " around younger girls falling pregnant, they took into account the possibility that the girl may not have known till after the third month that she was pregnant or she may have not been brave enough to tell anybody. This led the Justices to include the second trimester in the decision on the viability of the fetus. They did not agree that the third trimester be included, because by this time the fetus is a viable entity that could survive in the world if it was born.

Roe was pregnant in 1969, but by the time the verdict was announced in January 1973, she had already given birth for the third time and had given the baby up for adoption again. Ultimately, the woman whose case changed abortion laws for almost fifty years did not really benefit from the landmark ruling. But through her bravery, she changed the lives of millions of women.

Doe v. Bolton

This particular case was presented before the Supreme Court around the same time as the Roe v. Wade case. The Doe v. Bolton case was heard in a court in Georgia and was based on different circumstances for the woman concerned. Georgia law allowed abortion in cases of rape, deformities of the fetus, or if the fetus posed a risk to the health of the mother. There were additional stipulations that required the woman to have the written approval of three separate physicians to certify the pregnancy would pose a risk to the health of the mother, or that the fetus was severely deformed physically or mentally, or that the woman in question had been a victim of rape or incest. An abortion would only be sanctioned if the woman was a resident in the state of Georgia.

Mary Doe, a name used by the court to allow anonymity, sued the Attorney General of Georgia Arthur Bolton. Doe was nine weeks pregnant. Her lawyer presented to the courts that Doe had a neuro-chemical disorder and argued that her pregnancy be terminated. The lawyer claimed that Doe and her husband would have to discontinue having sex to stop her from becoming pregnant in the future.

The Georgia Court declared in October 1970 that the restrictions part of the law was unconstitutional, but upheld the physician's approval, and that she had to be a resident of Georgia. Doe appealed to the Supreme Court under a statute permitting the bypass of the circuit appeals court. After the Roe v. Wade victory, the Georgia abortion laws also fell away. Abortion was declared a constitutional right.

Abortion Data and Law Post-1973

In 2022, Ryan Nguyen from The Seattle Times compiled stories from readers on how Roe v. Wade affected their lives. Here is part of one:

> In my opinion, to be "pro-life" means to be committed to all people, including the women who become pregnant. The riskiest thing a woman ever does during her reproductive years is to carry a pregnancy to term. Each and every woman deserves to make that choice for herself and to receive safe care, whatever her decision is. It is a decision that she should be able to make with the com-

passionate and scientific medical coun-
sel her doctor can give her.

One very wise pediatrician I met during
my training said something that stuck
with me all these years: All children deserve not just to be born. They deserve
to be planned, loved and cared for. We
must not return to the barbaric days
before women could safely decide their
own futures, including if and when to
have children.

The elation felt by many pro-choice supporters over the Roe v. Wade 1973 ruling was not met
with the same enthusiasm and appreciation by
the pro-life lobbyists. The anti-abortion movement
swung into action almost at the hour of the verdict and began its campaign to derail the ruling.
The anti-abortionists were made up predominantly
of deeply religious members of churches—mainly
white Catholics, with a handful of people from other
religions. This movement started off small and over
the decades it began to draw a more considerable
following.

In the years after the Roe verdict, the Roman Catholic Church became very vocal about abortion and condemned it as murder and infanticide, since they believed that life begins at conception. Soon they were joined by fundamentalist Protestant church ministers and leaders. Monsignor McHugh helped form the National Conference of Catholic Bishops in 1966, and they formed the National Right to Life in 1968 to monitor developments in the abortion spectrum. They began to produce a newsletter in which they outlined plans to change the abortion laws. The National Right to Life Committee (NRLC) held its first meeting of anti-abortion leaders in 1970 in Chicago, Illinois. The establishment of this committee set in motion the chain reaction of events that led to the overturning of the Roe v. Wade 1973 ruling in 2022 (Karrer, 2011).

Any discussion about the sanctity of life and the fetus is going to elicit passionate responses, especially when it involves people's faith and religious beliefs. With the backing of the churches, the war between the pro-life and pro-choice groups was declared. Pro-life groups launched their attack by lobbying the relevant political groups and state senators in the bid to change the constitution with a Right to Life Amendment. Their bid made its way to Congress, but did not garner enough support. There was a reaction from the pro-choice camp which set up its own lobby and action groups such as National Abortion Rights Action League. The pro-choice groups have been living with dread that the tide could turn depending on the political leanings of the time.

The NRLC eventually splintered into smaller groups such as the Right to Life Crusade and the American Life League (ALL). These splinter groups have representative groups in many states, and they rally support and convert many to their way of thinking. The first bullet that was successfully launched by the pro-life camp was the passing of the Hyde Amendment of 1976 which stopped the use of Medicaid for abortions.

The Hyde Amendment of 1976

This amendment forbids abortions to be carried out using the federal government's money to do so. The pro-choice camp believes this amendment represents systemic racism, as it disadvantages the poorest women in American society, that is, Black, Hispanic, Indigenous, or people of color. Medicaid, Medicare, and the Children's Health Insurance Program are all state-subsidized schemes for those that need assistance, but in 1976, the Hyde Amendment was passed and ruled out using these services for procuring an abortion. In making the amendment, the Supreme Court failed to consider its impact on impoverished and desperate young women.

The offer of Medicaid is usually for people who need assistance due to their low earnings, and this applies to women of color most. In 2019, women of childbearing age who were enrolled for Medicaid included 29% Black women, 25% Hispanic, 15% White, and 12% Asian (Guttmacher Institute, 2022). In recent statistics released by the Guttmacher Institute, there is evidence that 7.8 million women in the United States between the ages of 15-49 are on Medicaid and will not qualify for abortions. Of this number, more than half of these women are women of color. The Hyde Amendment affects federal state workers like those in the military, veterans, prisoners, and Native Americans who are on Medicaid.

The terrible injustices that arose with the Hyde Amendment ruined lives. One example is the case of Rosie who was a single mother raising a daughter and trying to obtain her nursing degree in 1977. She happened to be pregnant and needed an abortion, but she could not get it done legally in the United States because of the Hyde Amendment. She traveled to Mexico to have an abortion. She died on

October 3, 1977 and became the first victim of the amendment.

In 1980, in Harris v. McRae, the Supreme Court upheld the Hyde Amendment, stating that women's constitutional rights were not violated by the ban on federal funding for abortions, even if the abortion was medically essential for the woman's health.

The amendment affects people across 34 states and people who live in the District of Columbia. In a survey undertaken by the Guttmacher Institute (2017), the average cost of abortion when comparing 808 clinics was around $550. This is an exorbitant amount of money for a woman eking out a living, working full time for a minimum wage. By the time she has earned enough money to pay for the abortion, her pregnancy may be out of the viability phase. If she is forced to continue with the pregnancy, she is condemned to live in poverty for longer than most and will probably lose her job. It is an appalling state of affairs for millions of poor women whose lives are deemed unimportant when compared to an unborn fetus.

Planned Parenthood v. Casey (1992)

This case was a complicated one that challenged the rulings of the Roe v. Wade verdict with regard to the strict trimester ruling. As a result, the court reviewed the strict trimester arrangement and also established that women had the right to choose to abort before viability. The Planned Parenthood v. Casey case raised the following:

- Informed consent: The woman had to be given notice 24 hours before the abortion about the status of the fetus, that the abortion could be bad for her, and to get her consent.

- Spousal notice: he had to get spousal permission.

- Parental consent: Minors had to have the permission of at least one parent or go through the courts.

- Medical emergency definition: The challenge to what constitutes an emergency.

- Reporting requirements: Certain reporting procedures would be imposed.

This was the first case to try and overturn the Roe v. Wade verdict. The pro-life sector realized that two of the more liberal Justices had left— Marshall and Brennan. They had been replaced by Justices appointed by President Bush Senior—Souter and Thomas. They were both deemed fairly conservative. This meant that the Supreme Court was left with eight conservative republican Justices and only one Democrat-appointed judge Justice White.

The Supreme Court ruled the following:

- Women had the right to abortion prior to viability which the Justices believed should be around 20-24 weeks. They felt the advances in medical science and technology had established viability around this time.

- The state had the right to impose restrictions after the viability period except in cases where the health of the mother became affected.

- The state could impose restrictions to protect the health of the mother or the health of the fetus.

- The court rejected the spousal consent clause stating that this gave too much power to the husband over the wife.

- The court upheld the other conditions of the 24-hour waiting period, parental consent, reporting requirements, and medical emergencies definition.

President George Bush also issued a "gag rule" that prevented workers in federally run facilities to discuss abortion as a solution. This was overturned when President Clinton took over in 1993.

Planned Parenthood was founded in 1916 to provide safe options for women with regard to pregnancy, contraceptives, advice, and abortions. Millions of women have been assisted by qualified staff at these centers. However, they have become targets of the pro-life movement. Anti-abortion placards and demonstrations are a regular feature outside the clinics and there have been reports of bombs being placed at the clinics by extreme pro-life groups.

It is obvious that the rules, laws, and statutes around abortion in the United States lie in the hands of the Supreme Court Justices and the lobbyists who drive the change. The battle will continue to rage between the pro-life and pro-choice groups as long as women are not supported by the men who impregnate them.

The 1990s to 2000s

During this time, there was growing support for the pro-life movement by the republican leaders who needed to garner votes and pandered to the call by the conservative views on anti-abortion. The pro-life groups are not a substantial group, yet they have had a powerful impact on the psyche of the people, and there are more pro-choice defections across the line. This was evidenced by Jane Roe who began as pro-choice and crossed the line to the other side in later years. Many pro-life advocates are now becoming actively involved in politics and are beginning to occupy positions in government to make the changes that they believe in. During the years following Casey, state and local legislatures passed more laws to restrict abortion, and the Supreme Court has more often upheld them.

Stenberg v. Carhart (2000)

This case emanated from Nebraska which prevented "partial birth" abortions. These refer to abortions in which a doctor delivers a living, unborn fetus—this process willfully results in the death or killing of the said fetus. Today this process is known as Dilation and Curettage (D&C), or Dilation and Extraction (D&E or D&X). This method is usually performed in the second trimester of pregnancy. Any doctor who was found doing these procedures was guilty of a felony which could result in the revocation of their license. The court ruled that if no other safe method could be found, then the method could not be banned.

However, nothing is permanent in the battle between the pro-life and pro-choice movements, because three years later under the leadership of President Bush, Congress signed into law the Partial-Birth Abortion Act of 2003. The Supreme Court overruled the Stenberg v. Carhart pronouncement in 2007 in Gonzales v. Carhart and banned the practice of partial abortions. The reason for this pendulum swing was the change once more of two new Justices in 2006, Roberts and Alito.

What becomes transparent in the observation of these to-and-fro Supreme Court stances is the change has to do with the people involved in the decision making. It is the politicization of the Supreme Court based on the Justices appointed by the president in office and the swing to the left or right. Supreme Court Justice Ruth Ginsburg was incensed by the ruling in the Gonzales v. Carhart ruling and said (Baker, 2020):

> Today's decision is alarming... It tolerates, indeed applauds, federal intervention to ban nationwide a procedure found necessary and proper in certain cases by the American College of Obstetricians and Gynecologists (ACOG). It blurs the line, firmly drawn in Casey, between pre-viability and post-viability abortions. And, for the first time since Roe, the Court blesses a prohibition with no exception safeguarding a woman's health.

Ginsburg, who was a champion of gay rights, women's rights, and rights of the poor and marginalized, was aware of the slow erosion of the Roe decision and how the Supreme Court was edging toward greater restrictions on abortions.

The Supreme Court passed the law after the Bellotti v. Baird (1979) case, which stated that minors had to obtain parental consent to get an abortion, together with the proviso that states enforced a "judicial bypass option" where the young women involved could petition a judge for permission if they did not want to let their parents know. The Court would be able to decide whether the young woman displayed the psychological strength and maturity to undertake the procedure. On September 16, 1988, a young 17-year-old Indiana teenager died from sepsis and pneumonia after a back alley abortion. She became the poster child for being the first person to die of illegal abortion as a result of the parental consent clause. Rebecca's parents began campaigning against the law, but with little effect.

The Unborn Victims of Violence Act of 2004

The bill was signed into law in 2004 by President Bush. It refers to a crime against a fetus, known as feticide. It has criminalized the deliberate murder of a fetus or the pregnant mother in a list of about

60 different crimes. United States law defines the child "in utero" as a member of the homo sapiens species at any stage in the womb. It granted legal personhood to the fetus, and this was a victory for the pro-life contingent. The bill was known as the Laci and Connor Law because of the murder of Laci Peterson, the mother who was killed while pregnant with her son-to-be Connor Peterson. The husband was convicted of double homicide after this became law. This was strongly opposed by the pro-choice people who challenged the notion that the fetus can be construed as a person.

In 2006, the youngest fetus to survive outside the womb was born in Hawaii at 21 weeks and 3 days, and this altered perceptions of the viability of a fetus. It spurred pro-life supporters to question destroying a living entity too soon.

The Affordable Care Act (ACA) was made law in 2010 and it allows individual states to limit or prohibit abortions in health insurance plans through an exchange. Since then, 26 states have restricted health plans within the exchange from allowing abortions. The ACA allows insurance providers to refuse to pay or refer for abortion services. Forty-six states have such laws. Despite this limitation, there are organizations like the Center for Reproductive Rights and the Guttmacher Institute that continue to fight for insurance coverage for all maternal care and abortion rights. There are also several private abortion funds that have been set up to try to help with the restrictions on abortion funding.

According to the Guttmacher Institute, federal states have been putting more and more anti-abortion legislation in place. There were more than 1,000 restrictions placed on abortions between 2011 to 2019 and seem to increase with the Obama presidency. Some of the laws enacted include looking at the fetus's gestation, the race of the mother, genetic anomalies, banning certain abortion methods, counseling the pregnant woman, imposing waiting periods, forcing the pregnant woman to view an ultrasound of the fetus, and insisting on Targeted Regulation of Abortion Providers (TRAP) regulations.

TRAP regulations attempt to apply irrational requirements for clinics or facilities that provide abortion services. An example would be to make certain unrealistic

recommendations for the size of the corridor in the hospital, or that the procedure must be performed at a hospital with prescribed mandates that such hospitals may refuse to grant. Pro-choice activists declare that these TRAP laws are deliberate attempts to derail the abortion rights of women and delay the procedure. It is also to make life for the service providers so difficult that they would close down businesses and bring an end to abortions. The Guttmacher Institute indicates that as of 2020, 26 states have TRAP policies in place.

The Whole Women's Health v. Hellerstedt (2016) was enacted in Texas and stipulated physicians who performed abortions needed to acquire admitting privileges at a hospital close by with specialized facilities and ambulatory surgical centers. The Supreme Court ruled that such restrictions violated the 14th Amendment because they created an undue burden on access to abortion by placing too many obstacles in the way of women seeking an abortion. Despite this decision, the Fifth Court of Appeals upheld a similar type of law in Louisiana, but the Supreme Court ruled against this in June Medical Services v. Russo.

The appointment of Donald Trump as President set the stage for the changes that would emerge. He appointed two Justices to the Supreme Court, Gorsuch and Kavanaugh. These Justices are very conservative in their views and known as fervent anti-abortion policy makers and activists. Once this had been done, the state legislators began to impose more stringent anti-abortion legislation. Some of these laws are listed:

- In 2019, seven states banned abortion in the first trimester.

- Georgia, Kentucky, Louisiana, Mississippi, and Ohio instituted fetal heartbeat bills that do not allow abortions after six weeks when the fetal heartbeat is discernible.

- Missouri passed an eight-week ban on abortions.

- Alabama put an end to all abortions except when a mother's life was in danger or in cases of rape and incest.

- In 2020, Arkansas enacted four new abortion restrictions such as a ban on D&E procedures, or abortion providers had to notify law enforcement officials when conducting an abortion on a teenager under 17 years.

- In 2020, during the COVID-19 pandemic, non-essential procedures were halted in many hospitals. Anti-abortion policymakers in 12 states attempted to close down abortion clinics and declared them as a non-essential procedure. These kinds of anti-abortion stances were prevalent in Texas, Alabama, Iowa, Tennessee, Ohio, and Oklahoma. Many medical organizations combined to fight these rising injustices. They included the American College of Obstetricians and Gynecologists, and the Society for Family Planning. They asserted that abortions were essential healthcare and should be accessible to women during the pandemic because they had a profound effect on the health and well-being of women.

• There was a move to pass "personhood laws" to declare that zygotes, embryos, and fetuses were persons and to criminalize abortions. States such as Alabama, Kansas, and Missouri have considered such legislation and have passed them.

• The Hyde Amendment Law restricted using state money to fund abortions. Medicaid will only cover abortions in the case of rape, incest, or if the mother's life is at risk. Thirty-four states still apply the Hyde Amendment. As a result, restrictions were placed on 7.9 million women in 2017. Research has shown that 55% of women of reproductive age who have Medicaid are living in states that promote the Hyde Amendment and do not have cover for abortion. Fifty-one percent of these women are women of color (All Above All, 2022). Studies indicate that when restrictions are placed on women dependent on Medicaid, one in four women who do not manage to get an abortion are forced to have the baby. This places a huge burden on her if she is barely managing to scrape a living or is unemployed. It is a vicious cycle for women belonging to the lower socio-economic groups because they do not have disposable income, depend on Medicaid, and qualify for insurance that does not cover abortions. This leads to them not getting reliable contraception and becoming pregnant. They are being forced by the state to have another mouth to feed, and the poverty just keeps rolling onto that unwanted child that is now stuck in the same cycle of poverty.

There have been a lot of women of color who joined together to ask for the Hyde Amendment to be repealed so that women disadvantaged by the act may access funding for abortions once more. In 2015, congresswomen Barbara Lee (California), Jan Schakowsky (Illinois), Ayanna Pressley (Massachusetts), Diane DeGette (Colorado), and senators Tammy Duckworth (Illinois), Patty Murray (Washington), and Mazie Hirono (Hawaii) instituted the Each Woman Act which sought to ensure every woman who required an abortion would be able to get one, irrespective of her social stature, employment status, race, age, or whether she has insurance or not. The All Above All campaign unites organizations and individuals to lift the bans on public insurance coverage for abortions. The Helms Amendment passed in 1973 forbids the use of United States foreign aid to fund abortions. This was cemented by the Mexico City Policy that was introduced by Ronald Reagan in 1984 which forbade foreign NGOs to provide abortion services if they wanted any United States health funding. In literature, this policy is called the "global gag rule." This rule has been in place under every single republican president and repealed by every democratic president. Donald Trump, the last republican president, extended the rule to all United States global health assistance.

Although this global gag rule is in place, it has been taken on by some in Congress and opposed by Senator Shaheen and Representative Lowey in 2019 who introduced the Global Health, Empowerment, and Rights Act (HER) to repeal the global gag rule. In 2020, Representative Schakowsky introduced the Abortion is Health Care Everywhere Act of 2020 to repeal the Helms Amendment.

Title X clinics perform a very important function across the United States, offering free or low-cost reproductive health services to low-income women. They are able to do this because they used to obtain funding from the federal government. In 2019, the Trump administration imposed a domestic gag rule which insisted that Title X clinics receiving federal funding were banned from referring patients for abortions. This has resulted in Title X clinics having to reduce their capacity.

Extremism and Violence

The pro-life movement consists of many extremists whose religious fervor pushes them to engage in scare tactics to threaten abortion clinics and counseling centers. This has led to a shocking use of manipulation, violence, and terror campaigns against doctors, nurses, and clinics, and they harass patients who dare to enter. There is a constant barrage of placard demonstrations, stalking of patients and doctors, threatening phone calls, death threats, blockades across entrances to clinics, physical violence, and damage to property. In the 1990s eleven people were killed—two clinic workers, four doctors, a security guard, a clinic escort, and two people who were at the clinic. Many others have been injured in confrontations with extremist pro-life supporters.

Bergengruen (2022) states that, "Violence against abortion providers rose significantly in 2021, according to a report last month from NAF, which has been tracking this

data for 45 years. Assaults of abortion-clinic employees and patients increased 128% year-over-year, while stalking leaped 600% and bomb threats jumped 80%."

There is a slow invasive war that has been brewing since 1973. It has been dependent on the political party that is in power and then the pendulum starts to swing. When the conservative Republicans dominate the Supreme Court, then the swing is to stringent anti-abortion legislation such as the Hyde Amendment, and when it is a swing to the left, there are more liberal laws and the pro-choice advocates benefit. The federal government responded to this violence by passing the Freedom of Access to Clinics Entrance Act of 1994. This act was to curtail the damage done to abortion and reproductive clinics. So far, 14 states have instituted laws to protect clinics and prevent pro-life supporters from blocking entrances, threatening staff, causing damage, threatening phone calls, carrying weapons, or causing any other related disturbances around abortion clinics. Despite this government intervention, the intimidation has not ceased.

Telemedicine Abortion

This type of abortion uses pills to assist with ending a pregnancy with telemedicine, allowing health care providers to reach their patients via telephone conversations and videoconferencing. This is FDA approved and used during the first 10 weeks of gestation. The medications used are misoprostol and mifepristone. The pill is ingested and is safe up to 12 weeks. According to statistics produced by the

Guttmacher Institute, in 2017 this type of pregnancy is most common in about 40% of all abortions and 60% for up to 10 weeks' gestation. With the onset of COVID-19 in early 2020, this type of abortion was the most popular. Despite the safety and support available through this type of abortion, many states prohibit telemedicine channels of accessing abortion. Eighteen states still require physical contact between the clinician and patient when the abortion pill is prescribed, while 33 states require the pill to be prescribed by a qualified physician.

In 2000, the FDA used the Risk Evaluation and Mitigation Strategy (REMS) to restrict the distribution of mifepristone after pressure from the pro-life camp. REMS restricts the circulation of medications or drugs that have serious safety concerns. It stipulates that mifepristone must be issued in person under the supervision of a qualified health care provider that has to be registered with the drug company. There has been opposition to this in some states such as Hawaii, Oregon, New Mexico, Georgia, Washington, Colorado, New York, Iowa, Maine, Illinois, Minnesota, Maryland, and Montana, since 2016, where they have implemented *Gynuity* and *TelAbortion* that provides medication abortion via videoconferencing without an in-person visit.

During the COVID-19 pandemic, with the call for social distancing and quarantining, many people challenged the REMS restrictions on medication abortions and telemedicine. On March 20, 2020, California Attorney General Xavier Becerra, together with 21 other state attorneys sent correspondence to the FDA to consider wavering the REMS enforcement of telemedicine and medication abortion. A temporary suspension of the REMS was allowed in Maryland.

Abortion Statistics Since Roe 1973

The most comprehensive statistics about abortions available are from the CDC and the Guttmacher Institute (GI). These institutions use different methods to collate these figures. The CDC acquires its data from organizations that volunteer their information to the central health agency for the majority of the states, but the recent amounts do not include California, New Hampshire, or Maryland.

The Guttmacher Institute compiles its data by making contact with all abortion providers in the United States. It uses questionnaires and health data. For states that do not respond, estimates are included. For this reason, the GI has higher data than the

CDC. The following table was compiled by christia nliferesources.com.

Abortion Data per Decade Since 1973

The 1970s

The data from the CDC and Guttmacher Institute show a drastic increase in abortion rates. This was probably because it was the first time that abortions were legal and were being properly documented (NRLC, 2022).

Year	GI	CDC

The 1980s

There was a similar trend to the 1970s with a continuing increase in abortion numbers.

Year	GI	CDC

The 1990s

For the first decade since Roe 1973, there is an observable reduction in abortion rates across the United States. Some of the reasons for this change could be education around sexuality and access to good quality support from organizations like Planned Parenthood.

The 2000s

Abortion numbers are still in a steady decline through the early 2000s.

The 2010s

For the first time the numbers actually drop below a million. The trend that is dominant is representative of the changes in the social and educational landscape. With access to education, contraceptives, and abortions being legal, women had more options and wanted much more out of life than staying home and having children.

* Excludes NH, CA, and at least one other state
** NRLC projection for calculation

From the early '90s, abortion numbers continued to decline up to the present time. We will no longer have accurate abortion numbers from 2022, because in states where abortion is banned or restricted, there will be no data to count the abortions occurring under the radar. Abortion numbers will be higher in states that continue to offer abortions, as women will cross state boundaries to acquire them.

In the graph below, it is quite clear that before Roe v. Wade 1973, there was little documentation of abortion numbers. From 1973, there was an alarming increase, but this was due to the legalization of abortion. From 1973 up to the early 1990s the numbers of abortions escalated across the United States. From the early '90s, there was a visible decline in the number of abortions, and this trend continued up to 2021.

Associated Press Statistics

Using data from CDC and GI, Associated Press (2022) issued the following statistics on abortion:

- Abortion rates: Abortion numbers have been in decline since 1.6 million in 1990, and there has been a decrease in pregnancy rates as well. The Guttmacher Institute collated 160 pregnancies per

1000 among women in their 20s in 1973, while in 2017 there were 110 per 1000 which was a lot less. When assessing data from GI and CDC, there was a steady increase in abortions from 1973 through the 1980s and early 1990s. In 1991, the GI reflected more than 1.5 million abortions compared to 2020 when it was 930,160. The CDC recorded 1 million in 1991 and 629,898 in 2020. It is apparent that there is quite a huge discrepancy between these two sets of data.

- Age of women: There were 11.4 abortions per 1,000 women aged 15 to 44 in 2019, compared to 16.3 per 1,000 in 1973. Women in their 20s constituted 57% of all abortion patients in 2019 according to the CDC, 31% in their 30s, teens 13-19 made up 9%, and women in their 40s constituted 4%.

- Gestation period of abortions: 94% of abortions were done before 13 weeks of pregnancy. Six percent took place between 14 and 20 weeks, and 1% occurred at 21 weeks or more. According to the CDC, the data was extrapolated from 42 states and New York City.

- Abortion procedures: Forty-four percent of United States abortions are done with pills rather than medical procedures. That rate has been increasing since 2000 when mifepristone, the main drug used, was approved by the Food and Drug Administration.

- Surgery abortions: Fifty-six percent of United States abortions are done with some type of surgery.

- Complications: Two percent of abortions result in some form of complication.

- Abortion mortality rates: The CDC calculates the mortality rate due to abortion every five or six years. When observing fatality rates due to abortion, the

lowest rate was between 2013 and 2018 at 0.4% per 100,000; from 1973 to 1977 it was 2.1% per 100,000; from 1978 to 1982 it was 0.8% per 100,000; from 1993-1997

it was 0.5% per 100,000. In 1982, there were 2,908 abortion service providers that included physicians, doctors, and clinics. In 2017, there were 1,587 facilities which showed a significant drop. Clinics make up 51% of service providers.

- Out-of-state abortions: In 1972, 41% of all abortions in Washington D.C. or the 20 states that provided such information to the CDC were performed on women

outside their state. In 1973, the corresponding figure was 21% in Washington D.C. and the 41 states. In 1974, it was 11% in Washington D.C. and the other 43 states.

- Race and abortions: Almost 3/4 of all abortions in 2019 were amongst Black and White women. The CDC data on race is from 30 areas that reported race and ethnicity. The following was derived from the CDC report on 29 states and Washington D.C. concerning women between the ages of 15 to 44:

○ Black women had the highest rate with almost 24 abortions per 1,000 women.

○ White women had the lowest, at almost seven per 1,000 women.

○ There were 23.8 abortions per 1,000 non-Hispanic Black women.

○ There were 11.7 abortions per 1,000 Hispanic women.

○ There were 6.6 abortions per 1,000 non-Hispanic White women.

○ There were 13 abortions per 1,000 women of other races or ethnicities.

• Prior births before an abortion: Most women who have abortions—about 60%—have at least one child, according to CDC's 2019 data.

• More single women procure abortions: In 2019, 85% of women who procured abortions were single women and 15% were married.

• The number of abortions: The CDC report concluded the following statistics based on 43 states and New York city, focusing on the number of abortions procured by women in the United States.

Amongst the 58% of women who had induced abortions in 2019

- ○ it was their first abortion
- ○ for 24% of the women, it was their second attempt
- ○ it was the third abortion for 11%
- ○ it was 8% for the fourth or higher

Impact of Abortion on Crime

John Donahue and Steven Levitt suggested in a paper they co-wrote in 2001 that legalizing abortion in 1973 would have a direct impact on the crime rate years later. They said:

> When a steady state is reached roughly twenty years from now, the impact of abortion will be roughly twice as great as the impact felt so far. Our results suggest that all else equal, legalized abortion will account for persistent declines of 1 percent a year in crime over the next two decades.

Twenty years later, Donahue and Levitt revised their original hypothesis and used 17 years of data to verify their theory. They found that crime fell

20% between 1997 and 2014, due to abortion being legalized. When they looked at the cumulative effect of crime over the years, they estimated there was a 50% decline in crime since the early 1990s.

Donahue and Levitt had a very simple theory. They believed that unwanted children were more likely to be involved in crime as they got older, "but an unwanted child who was never born would never have the opportunity to enter his criminal prime, 15 or 20 years later."

SUPREME COURT DECISION 2022

Whatever the exact scope of the coming laws, one result of today's decision is certain: the curtailment of women's rights, and of their status as free and equal citizens... With sorrow—for this court, but more, for the many millions of American women who have today lost a fundamental constitutional protection—we dissent.

This was the statement made by the three Democrat Justices Stephen Breyer, Sonia Sotomayor, and Elena Kagan who dissented on the overturning of the Roe v. Wade ruling of 1973. For almost 39 years, there has been an ongoing tension in the state courts, state legislation, Supreme Court, clinics, and hospitals, between pro-life and pro-choice supporters— allover an issue that has divided people in America to such an extent that it has resulted in polarization and division in every quarter. It has impacted presidents, the wealthy, the poor, the fanatics, and the non-believers.

No matter what stance you take, you cannot ignore that we inevitably end up being influenced by our moral sense of what is right and wrong. As thousands of protesters thronged outside the Supreme Court waiting for the outcome, there were already pro-life and pro-choice protests going on all around the United States, sparking doubt, fear, and outrage. A leak from within the Supreme Court already had people on edge. Young women who were pro-choice were especially incensed as they slowly saw the future grow bleak. When Justice Alito read the verdict, millions were despondent. Representing the six republican Justices he said, Roe "usurped the power to address a question of profound moral and social importance that the Constitution unequivocally leaves for the people."

Justice Alito and the other conservative Justices believed that the Roe v. Wade decision was "egregiously wrong" and "on a collision course with the Constitution from the day it was decided." Many conservatives in the legal profession believe that the Constitution does not relate in any way to allowing abortion. One's right to privacy does not necessarily mean consent to commit murder.

In one fell swoop, the country was changed, due largely to the ideological standing of six Justices who were strategically placed to create that change with political meanderings that have been in place behind the political and funding scenes. The ruling is not a surprise, because since 1973, there has been constant chipping away at the liberties that came with the legalization of abortion. There were several cases over the years that were taken before the courts with many states manipulating the system.

Dobbs v. Jackson Women's Health Organization

In 2018, Mississippi passed the Gestational Age Act which forbade abortion after 15 weeks except in cases where there was fetal abnormality or the mother's life was at risk. This meant that once the fetus has a heartbeat—the organs are developing into a recognizable human form and there is a quickening or discernible movement of the fetus—abortion cannot take place. Jackson Women's Health Organization, an abortion clinic, together with service provider Dr. Carr-Ellis, filed a suit asking for a temporary restraining order against the enforcement of the Gestational Age Act. The district court granted them a temporary restraining order.

Thomas Dobbs was a Mississippi Health Officer who had petitioned the court arguing that with technological advancements such as ultrasounds, 3-D imaging, and intrauterine fetal observation, it was possible to observe that the fetus at 12 weeks old was already a fully sensing being that deserved to be protected, and that the Gestation Age Act was constitutional. The district court ordered a fact-finding team to determine if the 15-week mark was before or after quickening or viability. Dobbs was not particularly pleased because he had brought an expert medical witness who was not allowed to testify in front of the court. The witness was supposed to testify that a fetus could feel pain after 15 weeks.

Dobbs filed certiorari, which called for a higher court to hear the case. He challenged the assertion that the Constitution allowed the right of abortion or even mentions abortion at all. On these grounds, he contended that a state is allowed to ban abortions. Dobbs argued that the use of the word "liberty" in the Due Process Clause of the 14th Amendment does not relate to the right to abortion at all, but is rather related to United States history and tradition.

Women's Health reacted to Dobbs's reasoning with the salvo that in the 14th Amendment, the word "liberty" protects a woman's right to possession of her own body and the right to decide what is right for her own body.

One of the strongest points that Dobbs made was that the right to abortion was the only constitutional right that involved taking a life. Dobbs strongly lobbies for giving women access to what they need to prevent pregnancy, such as contraceptives and health care which would reduce abortions and protect women.

Women's Health countered that a women's right to choose when to have children was an individual's right to body autonomy. They also challenged Dobbs's argument that contraception and health care would deem abortion unnecessary, because realistically speaking, access to these services is not possible for everyone, and it's certainly not affordable for women with low income. Women's Health believes that gender equality has not been reached and women have a right to decide for themselves. It is essential for women to have access to the resources that would allow their equal status in the economy and society.

Dobbs had the support of Concerned Women for America (CWA) who believed that the Supreme

Court had failed women by not understanding the adverse effect of abortions on women and that access to abortions ensures equality. They rebuked the court for assuming that pro-choice groups were representative of all women in the United States. Dobbs also enjoyed the support of the Roman Catholic Dioceses of Jackson and Biloxi, Mississippi that challenged the Supreme Court's stance on abortion when it had a duty to protect the right to life and that life was sacred and began at conception. The Jewish Pro-Life Foundation took a similar stance and declared that abortion is an anathema to the Torah and that life begins at conception.

There were organizations that supported the Women' Health perspective. The National Asian Pacific Women's Forum (NAPW) contends that it is essential to protect the emotional well-being and economic stature of Asian-American and Pacific Islander women residing in America who encounter tremendous obstacles such as racism and do not need another form of discrimination with limitations on what women can or cannot do with their own bodies. The National Women's Law Centre agrees with the NAPW that access to abortions protects women's fiscal well-being, health, and autonomy. They believe that the change in the laws in Mississippi will exacerbate the position of other groups like minorities, people of color, homosexuals, and transsexuals. It will degrade the right to self-determination. The Catholics for Choice supported the Women's Health plight because they believe that the right to choose is a woman's prerogative and state that there is no acceptable teaching in the biblical texts about when life begins or when the fetus can be classified as a viable entity.

As we assess the arguments presented by Dobbs and Women's Health, it becomes increasingly clear that the polarization is based on valid moral, ethical, social, and economic realities on both sides of the spectrum.

Up to the States

With the overturning of Roe and Casey, it is now left up to individual states to decide on how they will regulate abortion law. From 1973, Roe instituted a legal framework within which all states could formulate these laws, and the removal of Roe dismantled all that had been put in place. Now, there are various ways individual states are handling the issues of abortion:

• Abortions banned: As soon as Roe was overturned, 13 states that had trigger laws immediately banned abortions. They were Wyoming, Tennessee,

Arkansas, Idaho, Kentucky, Louisiana, Mississippi, Missouri, North Dakota, Oklahoma, South Dakota, Texas, and Utah.

- Abortion legal: There are states where abortion has been declared legal at any stage of the pregnancy. These include Alaska, Colorado, New Jersey, New Mexico, Oregon, Vermont, and the District of Columbia.

- Abortion before viability: 18 states will allow abortion in the stage when the fetus is non-viable which is around 15 weeks. This means that a few more restrictions
will be imposed. These 18 states include California, Hawaii, Connecticut, Illinois, Delaware, Maine, Kansas, Maryland, Massachusetts, Nevada, Minnesota, New Hampshire, New York, North Carolina, Pennsylvania, Rhode Island, Virginia, and Washington.

- Pending decisions: There are six states that have abortion bans but have not enforced them since 1973, but could begin their stringent laws with the overturning of Roe. These states include Alabama, Arizona, Michigan, North Carolina, West Virginia, and Wisconsin.

- Possible ban on abortions: A few states had already put restrictions in place before the overturning of Roe and may restrict abortion completely.

These include Florida
  and Georgia.

Over the months after the overturning of Roe, there will be a clearer understanding of the extent to which each state will regulate its stance on abortion. It's unclear at this point how abortion law is going to be handled by the individual states, but it's going to be fairly complicated. What we know from pre-Roe is that the lives of women are going to be under scrutiny, that in some ways they will lose some of their basic rights and control over their own bodies, and they may have travel restrictions imposed on them. All the gains made over the last 40 or so years will have been overturned, and the struggle will begin all over again. Those living in states that ban abortions will need to travel across state lines to acquire an abortion, and those who cannot afford to will resort to dangerous illegal abortions putting their lives at risk.

The Trump Effect

These were the triumphant proclamations of former President Donald Trump to the overturning of the Roe 1973 case (Feiner & Mangan, 2022):

"The biggest win for life in a generation!"

"... only made possible because I delivered everything as promised, including nominating and getting three highly respected and strong Constitutionalists confirmed to
the United States Supreme Court."

"... did not cave to the radical left Democrats, their partners in the fake news media, or the RINOs [Republicans in Name Only] who are likewise the true, but silent enemy of the people."

"These major victories prove that even though the radical left is doing everything in their power to destroy our country, your rights are being protected, the country is being defended, and there is still hope and time to save

America! I will never stop fighting for
the great people of our nation!"

"It was my great honor to do so!"

Trump was quick to take full credit for this new
verdict because his strategic placement of three
conservative Justices resulted in the change. Trump
nominated Neil

Gorsuch, Brett Kavanaugh, and Amy Coney Barrett to the Supreme Court as Justices during his term
of office. Coney Barrett was appointed in 2020, just
a week before the presidential elections took place
and Trump was voted out of office. With the death
of Justice Ruth Ginsberg, Trump and his cohorts
rushed the decision through the Senate so that the
republican Justices would be in the majority to make
any crucial decisions.

Kavanaugh's appointment was also under a dark
veil because as he was nominated in 2018 by the
Trump administration, there were allegations of
sexual assault leveled at

him and a high school friend. He denied these
allegations and was installed as a Justice in the
Supreme Court to make pronouncements that
would affect women in the United States. It is laugh-

able that a president who was accused of similar misconduct appoints a Justice to the Supreme Court who was accused of similar crimes against women, and that together they decide what is to be in the *best interests of women* by allowing abortion to be banned wherever the people decide.

They were joined by two other conservative Justices on the panel. Together they managed to turn the decades-long tide in favor of the pro-life camp.

Gorsuch was nominated by Trump in 2017. Barack Obama nominated Merrick Garland in 2016 after the death of Justice Scalia, but the decision was not finalized because

Senate Leader Mitch McConnell refused to hold confirmation hearings. This dragging of feet has had a direct bearing on the outcome on June 24, 2022 when Roe v. Wade was reversed.

The Blue States vs. the Red States

This term was coined in the 2000 United States presidential election to refer to states where most of the voters seem to vote for one particular party—red for the Republican Party and blue for the Democratic Party. It harks back to an earlier time during the American Civil War when the blue north was seen as liberal and anti-slavery. Now, "red states" is used to refer to right-wing, conservative views and "blue states" refer to left-wing, more liberal views. Of course, this can differ within a state, its regions, and its rural and urban populations. There's a tendency to classify a state as blue or red depending on the greater number of votes received by a party, while disregarding the votes for the loser party. States do sometimes switch their category, like from 2000 to 2004, when some states changed their color. As of 2020, 35 out of 50 states have voted for the same party in every election (Wikipedia, 2022).

After the Roe overturning, there were a few red states that immediately banned abortions. They were Wyoming, Tennessee, Arkansas, Idaho, Kentucky, Louisiana, Mississippi, Missouri, North Dakota, Oklahoma, South Dakota, Texas, and Utah.

The blue states are Alaska, Colorado, New Jersey, New Mexico, Oregon, Vermont, and the District of Columbia.

There are states that are possibly purple and may allow abortions with restrictions. They are California, Hawaii, and Connecticut, Illinois, Delaware, Maine, Kansas, Maryland, Massachusetts, Nevada, Minnesota, New Hampshire, New York, North Carolina, Pennsylvania, Rhode Island, Virginia, and Washington.

Although political analysts have tried to demarcate red and blue states, it really can't be determined, because within red states there are blue cities and towns, and within blue states there exist red cities and towns. It's definitely a fluid and changing landscape that can swing with the dominant party in power at the time. Politics in America are like a pendulum, swinging right and left.

One of the states that is definitely red is Texas which had a trigger law that allowed it to reinstate a ban on abortions the day the Roe case was overturned; however, it was

temporarily blocked by a state court. Ohio has already instituted a ban on abortions after six weeks of gestation, while Arizona already had plans for a ban on abortion before 1973. Texas is going the whole nine yards and seeking to put women procuring abortions under surveillance, or prosecute doctors that may be involved in providing abortions.

In Cincinnati, Ohio, Mayor Pureval has begun to look at decriminalizing abortions so that law enforcement resources are not wasted on arresting women, doctors, nurses, and other workers that may be hounded for abortion-related crimes.

In Phoenix, Arizona, Mayor Gallego has no intention of criminalizing health care workers who are involved with abortions and voted to stop their law enforcement officers from arresting people involved with abortions. Other cities that had a pre-Roe ban on abortion have also taken measures to protect women needing abortions and their health care providers.

Despite all the attempts to decriminalize abortions within a red state, there are still steps that can be taken by certain officials within the government to derail these attempts. The state attorney's office and district attorneys could still seek to serve civil or criminal sanctions against people who play a role in the abortion sector. There are medical boards that could serve harsh penalties on health care workers if they transgress the rules of the board—they could revoke or suspend licenses.

IMPACT AND FALLOUT

P eople gathered at the Capitol building the day after the Supreme Court overturned Roe v. Wade. There were some who were in tears and looked despondent by the decision, while others were jubilant and overjoyed. The pro-life brigade was effusive in their victory with champagne bottles being popped and passed around. There were pro-life celebrants who crumbled to the ground, in tears of joy, when the court verdict was announced.

Pro-life Reaction

Rose King, one of the pro-life supporters who attended the rally organized by Texas Right to Life, a non-profit opposing abortion, commented that it was long overdue: "It's a real victory for life and for babies... we believe in the right for life and it's a victory for unborn babies" (Figuerero, 2022).

After the ruling, abortions were declared illegal in the state of Texas and in many others. Performing an abortion would be construed as a felony punishable by law. All abortion service providers were forced to close shop on June 24, 2022. Organizations like Planned Parenthood and woman's health clinics will have to stop performing abortions.

These were the words of another pro-life advocate (Figuerero, 2022), Kim Schwartz, a spokesperson for Texas Right to Life, who was celebrating at the Capitol buildings and called it a "celebration 50 years in the making."

For decades, we worked for this moment. Every day Americans prayed for this moment for years. Now we join together to thank God. The decision to overturn Roe

means that states will once again have the authority to defend preborn children from the slaughter of abortion. Now the battle will continue state by state, and we won't stop until every innocent human life is protected.

Macy Petty, a young woman who attended the rally at Capitol Hill, was on cloud nine when she heard the news and spoke about her work at pregnancy resource centers and the pain she has personally witnessed. She explained she counseled many women who had been to abortion clinics and were shattered by the treatment they received. They complained about being peddled abortion pills as a solution. Petty insists that pregnant women need support and understanding and an alternative that would benefit them most.

Another pro-life supporter interviewed by Schorr (2022) reports that she has heard many stories from women who have had abortions about the enduring pain that remains with them over time, and the deep regret and shame that accompanies abortion. This lady expressed sadness and empathy for the pro-choice supporters who were devastated by the decision. Her view is that there needs to be meaningful dialogue between both camps at this juncture, so that they can find some middle ground from which they could work, to help women who are in trouble and not cause them more pain and heartache.

Another young woman interviewed by Schorr at the rally was Kristin Turner who is currently the communications director of Progressive Anti-Abortion Uprising. Her personal story shows how one could start as a pro-choice advocate and end up a pro-life supporter. She talks of being entirely supportive of the pro-choice agenda when she was a teen, but completely switched her thinking after going through her own personal hell: "It wasn't until I started experiencing sexual abuse at the hands of a teacher that I thought I'd become pregnant at 16 with my abuser, and I researched what abortion was and saw the abortion procedure videos by Live Action."

Turner eventually decided that she could not condone taking the life of an innocent baby and changed her affiliation to pro-life.

Pro-choice Perceptions

In Jacksonville, Florida there were reactions across the spectrum from both anti-abortion and pro-abortion enthusiasts. News4Jax, a news channel, spoke to a few of the local people to find out their views (Harris, 2022). Pro-choice supporters believe that banning abortions is a step back. Alexis West was clear that only the individual in the body had the right to make a choice about that body. West told the news channel: "I am very upset because I don't think anyone should be able to dictate what we can do with our bodies except the woman who actually has the uterus."

Gilda Griffin-Thomas supports abortion rights and commented: "I feel like it's up to the female. If she wants to have an abortion, it's her right, than to have someone dictate what she should do with her own body."

Another pro-life supporter tells her story of suffering with severe mental illness and could not imagine herself remotely capable of caring a baby or successfully raising the child. When she became pregnant, she and her husband made the tough decision to end her pregnancy. She believes that women are all different and have varying challenges that must be taken into account. Looking back, she is grateful that she lived in a time when she had that choice. Can you imagine someone with a mental illness being forced to maintain a pregnancy, go through the rigors of childbirth, give a child up for adoption, or raise the child in a dysfunctional environment? The negative impact of such a situation makes us question whether there is a clear-cut decision that can be applied to all situations. Should there not be some middle ground and flexibility within the framework that allows women to still have some choice?

Pro-choice advocates have been vocal about the way the current status quo can be changed. They believe they can bring about the change at the polling station (NARAL Pro-Choice America, 2022):

The Supreme Court made it clear: They are overturning Roe and Casey. This is the end of our constitutionally-protected right to abortion. The impact on the real lives of real people will be devastating. The Supreme Court has given the green light to extremist state lawmakers who will waste no time springing into action to put in place total bans on abortion. And they won't stop there—the anti-choice movement and its political allies have already made it clear that they want to enact a nationwide ban on abortion. This decision is the worst-case scenario, but it is not the end of this fight. The 8 in 10 Americans who support the legal right to abortion will not let this stand.

There is an election in November, and extremist politicians will learn: when you come for our rights, we come for your seats.

NARAL Pro-Choice America has been supporting women's reproductive rights for the last fifty years. The organization is less than thrilled about the devastating impact this will have on women in

America. They spoke about the trigger laws and how 13 states jumped on banning abortions straight away. Anti-abortion lawmakers across the country have filed over 500 restrictions on abortions. Some of the restrictions include a ban on abortions after 15 weeks, stalking of abortion clinics and medical workers previously involved in conducting abortions, or medical restrictions on acquiring the abortion pill.

With the overturning of Roe, it's clear there is prejudice from the highest court in the land and that this influence will cascade down to the lower courts in the different states, especially the red states or more conservative areas of the country. The country will revert to the state it was in before 1973 when women's rights and their livelihoods were negatively affected. Women cannot count on the courts to protect their fundamental rights. NARAL believes that men and women across America who are keen to defend a woman's right to make decisions about her own body should elect the right candidates into power. It is the only way to turn the tide of the tyranny of conservatism and promote the liberties of the person and personal choice.

The pro-choice movement is not backing down, and in May 2022, NARAL, Planned Parenthood Action Fund, and Emily's List formed an alliance to collect $150 million for the 2022 mid-term elections to call for reproductive freedom and to elect leaders who will promote the values and majority of liberal Americans.

A lot of pro-life supporters work from their emotions and sense of morality, but sometimes we have to examine all the options and ramifications on the entire country and planet at the present moment. With mounting evidence that children who are unwanted end up in the welfare system, in foster care, or being brought up by single women who cannot afford to give them the care and love that a child needs, there will be a more far-reaching impact on the macro scale. We have looked at evidence that crime rates dropped after the legalization of abortion. Is America headed for an increase in crime in the next 20 years?

A day before the Roe ruling, there were conversations and debates taking place all over America and the world as to the repercussions of the possible overturning of the Roe 1973 ruling. One such conversation was heard on Fresh Air between host Terry Gross and Mary Ziegler, a law professor. Ziegler explained that with the Roe verdict in 1973 came a change in many other spheres of life in the United States. She likened it to an "interconnected web of decisions about privacy" and how it relates to self-determination and autonomy. She also spoke about how this single case allowed other significant changes to become more acceptable such as same-sex relationships and marriages or the decriminalization of sodomy.

Ziegler goes on to say (Gross, 2022):

> There are older decisions that Roe draws on that are closely tied to it, like decisions involving birth control, interracial marriage, with whom you can live, so your right to live with blood family, even in scenarios where zoning ordinances may make that difficult. All of those decisions touch on these ideas about the most personal, intimate, and consequential life decisions and insulating people from state interference with those decisions. So, if the Supreme Court is essentially saying the abortion right doesn't make sense because of how people would have thought at the time the 14th Amendment was written, we can reasonably ask whether the same logic could apply to the other rights in this interconnected web.

Ziegler raises a crucial concern about how all the gains that have been made by Americans could be under threat by the decision taken by Justice Alito and his peers to decide that the 14th Amendment does not include abortion rights or any other group rights within the framework at the time of the writing of the Constitution. There is a sense of "taking two steps forward and three steps back" in the handling of this decision by the Supreme Court. There has to be an understanding that change is the only constant in life. There has been a lot of change and progress since the original endorsement of the Constitution on September 17, 1787. Surely, there should be more amendments and tweaks to the Constitution to adapt to the changes that have swept across America and the world. We need to take into account the rights of individuals and their freedom of choice and self-determination and not impose the doctrines of churches, synagogues, temples, or mosques onto other people's personal freedoms and choices. Within our communities, there are many who do not believe in religion and morality, they believe in science, evolution and just being an evolved being. The Constitution needs to take into account the opinions of living, walking, breathing, and lucid beings, instead of trying to change the Constitution to declare the unborn fetus a person.

Projections of Roe Overturning in the Future

On perusal of the data on abortions, it's clear more than half the abortions in the United States are among women of color. The following data was extrapolated in 2019:

- 38% among Black women
- 33% among White women
- 21% among Hispanic women
- 7% from other races

Data used to extrapolate the findings was acquired from several sources (Artiga, Hill & Ranji, 2022):

- 2019 American Community Survey
- 2020 Behavioral Risk Factor Surveillance System
- 2021 Survey of Household Economics and Decision Making
- CDC, Morbidity, and Mortality Weekly Report on Abortion
- National Vital Stats
- 2017 CDC Natality Public Use File
- CDC WONDER Online Database

This is what we find in the surveys:

- Most abortions occur in the first trimester with the following splits: amongst Whites (81%), Hispanics (82%), and Blacks (76%). These findings show us that women of all races are having their abortions in the first trimester before the fetus is viable.

- Less than 10% of abortions occur in the second trimester, which indicates that women are heeding the suggestion to abort before quickening.

It's of note that women of color have a higher abortion rate. Why?

- They have limited access to health care.
- They have limited access to contraception.
- State reduction in midwifery services has resulted in poorer women not having the necessary counseling and support needed to prevent unwanted pregnancies.
- There is medical mistrust due to discrimination and forced sterilizations in the past.
- Economic issues such as unemployment, poorly paid jobs, lack of housing, poor safety and security, and poor quality education have a negative impact on a woman's ability to access resources and information to avoid pregnancy or raise a child that was unplanned.
- Lack of superior medical insurance. Most women of color usually receive Medicaid, and the Hyde Amendment has prevented them from being financed for abortions through Medicaid. Currently,

16 states have laws in place that insist that abortions are to be paid by the women themselves.

- Many women of color have immigration fears, as they may be in the country illegally and cannot cross state lines. Many Hispanic women cross the borders illegally and will rather get an illegal abortion than go to a state that offers legal, safe abortions.

- Women of color may have limited access to information, due to lack of internet access and lack of fluency in English.

- Women of color have a higher risk of dying due to complications from pregnancy.

- Stevenson (2021) estimates that a total ban on abortions in the United States would result in an increase of 33% in the deaths of Black women.

- Denying abortion to women of color has many social and economic implications such as poverty, debt, and poor credit ratings. They are forced to raise a whole human being with complex needs and wants that they may not be able to cope with.

- It could affect a young girl's or woman's ability to access higher education, and this will drive them further into poverty. Many women of color become pregnant in their teens and they are stuck in a vicious cycle of poverty because they are high school dropouts. Their poor quality of life is a direct result of their lack of skills or qualifications that would have assisted them to improve their standard of living.

- Children born to women of color who are forced to give birth to them may experience higher rates of poverty, they may have a lower level of education, have higher school dropout rates, grow up to earn lower wages, and may need to be put on public financial assistance. They are more likely to commit crimes, join gangs, take drugs, and experience health problems.

- Women of color may be at risk of being arrested for trying to procure abortions, especially in the red states. Texas and Oklahoma have laws in place to charge anyone who aids or abets in the performance of abortions with amounts starting at $10,000.

Clinicians and doctors may be wary of treating women with pregnancy-related issues such as miscarriages, for fear of being charged or arrested unfairly. Forcing women to carry their pregnancy to term will also flood the system with babies that need to be adopted and fostered. In poorer countries like South Africa where abortions are legal, poorer women cannot afford the abortion fee, and the amount of abandoned babies is high. Likewise, there could be an increase in the number of abandoned babies and children in the United States, which will have a direct impact on the foster care system and on state expenditure. At present, social workers have an already mammoth caseload. With the banning of abortions in many states, there will be an overburdening on these state departments. At the end of the day, taxpayers will have to fork out more money so that the state can support more unwanted children that poor women are forced to give birth to.

CONCLUSION

I n the writing of this book, there has been a lot of research done on both sides of the spectrum. It's very difficult to take a side because the arguments offered by each side independently can be really convincing. This is until you realize this argument is not some intellectual or doctrinal debate that somebody has to win. It's about that young woman struggling with an unwanted pregnancy that will ruin her life; it's about that 10-year-old child from Ohio who was raped by an adult; it's about the girl with Down's Syndrome who cannot cope with a pregnancy or bringing up a young baby; it's about the woman with a defective heart whose body cannot support a baby; it's about the girl who was on antibiotics and the pill did not work; it's about your sister who is menopausal and far too old to be a mother. It is an emotionally loaded issue that gets everyone riled up, but at the end of the day, that woman needs our support and not a judgment imposed by a dominant cohort of males who decide what a mother, daughter, sister, or friend does with her body.

The real problem is in the act of trying to give this issue a one-size-fits-all solution. The reality of the matter is that there are situations where abortion is, medically, the best choice for a mother. In others, it is not. However, once we make it a law that it cannot be done *except* in cases of [insert situation], we give the law room to be stretched and abused. For this reason, this should not be a law that is maintained on the Federal level. It should be relegated to the state legislatures, if anything.

As much as we defend the right of the person to exercise their rights over their own bodies, we cannot avoid the reality that we live in a social space that we share with other people who may differ in their perspective and ascribe to a differing worldview. We have to learn to co-exist and accommodate other moral perspectives as we navigate the stormy waters of the abortion debate. The conflicts that have raged through the centuries is an intersection of divergent thinking about religion and science, murder and morality, life and death, women and men, modern and antiquated thinking. The debate will continue to rage, depending on the socio-political landscape.

We want to thank you for taking the time to read our book. Whether you are pro-life or pro-choice, please take the time to leave a review on the basis of the writing, not on your personal preference of the idea of abortion. We worked very hard to compile the *history* of abortion in the US and we would appreciate any reviews that we can get. You can leave a review by clicking the link below (if you are on an ebook) or by scanning the QR code with your phone (if you are using a print version). The first 100 people to leave reviews will get their choice of one free paperback copy of this book or one free copy of any other book I have previously published or will publish in the coming months. All you need to do is email me with a screenshot of your review at porter62185@gmail.com and I will reach out to you to get your desired selection.

https//tinyurl.com/abortionpaperback

REFERENCES

- Abbott, K. (2012, November 27). *Madame Restell: The abortionist of Fifth Avenue.* Smithsonian Magazine. https://www.smithsonianmag.com/history/ madame-restell-the-abortionist-of-fifth-ave nue-145109198/

- Abort73.com. (2019). *U.S. abortion history.* Ab ort73.com. https://www.abort73.com/aborti on_facts/us_abortion_history/

- *Abortion - Abortion in English law.* (n.d.). Law. jrank.org. https://law.jrank.org/pages/445/A bortion-Abortion-in-English-law.html

- All Above All. (2022). *Each act fact sheet.* All Above All. https://allaboveall.org/resource/ each-act-fact-sheet/

- ANSIRH.org. (2020, April 16). *The harms of denying a woman a wanted abortion findings from the Turnaway Study.* ANSIRH.org. https://www.ansirh.org/sites/default/files/publications/files/the_harms_of_denying_a_woman_a_wanted_abortion_4-16-2020.pdf

- Aron, N. R. (2017, March 27). *The father of American gynecology fought to criminalize abortion in the 1850s.* Timeline. https://timeline.com/horatio-storer-criminal-abortion-c433606491da

- Artiga, S., Hill, L., & Ranji, U. (2022, July 15). *What are the implications of the overturning of Roe v. Wade for racial disparities?* KFF. https://www.kff.org/racial-equity-and-health-policy/issue-brief/what-are-the-implications-of-the-overturning-of-roe-v-wade-for-racial-disparities/

- Associated Press. (2022, May 3). *US abortion trends have changed since landmark 1973 ruling.* U.S. News and World Report. https://www.usnews.com/news/health-news/articles/2022-05-03/us-abortion-trends-have-changed-since-landmark-1973-ruling

- Bahn, J. (2022). *How does the Supreme Court work?* American Bar Association. https://www.americanbar.org/groups/young _lawyers/publications/after-the-bar/essenti als/how-does-the-supreme-court-work/#:~: text=Supreme%20Court%20justices%20hear %20oral

- Baker, C. (2020, September 14). *History of abortion in the U.S. - Our Bodies Ourselves.* Our Bodies Ourselves. https://www.ourbodiesourselves.org/book-e xcerpts/health-article/u-s-abortion-history/

- Bella, T. (2022, July 13). *Man charged in rape of 10-year-old girl who had to travel for abortion.* Washington Post. https://www.washingtonpost.com/politics/2 022/07/13/abortion-girl-rape-victim-arrest -ohio/

- Belz, E. (2022, July 1). *The pro-life movement faces blue state backlash. Christianity Today* https://www.christianitytoday.com/news/20 22/july/roe-wade-dobbs-abortion-blue-stat es-legislatures.html

- Bennett, D. M. (1878). Anthony Comstock: His Career of Cruelty and Crime, a chapter from *The champions of the church: Their crimes and persecutions*. New York: D. M. Bennett.

- Bergengruen, V. (2022, July 8). *Abortion protests see surge of armed demonstrators and far-right groups*. Time. https://time.com/6194085/abortion-protests-guns-violence-extremists/

- Brand, A. (2022, May 7). *"We cannot go back": People share their stories of abortion and access*. n b c n e w s . https://www.nbcnews.com/specials/abortion-and-access-stories-around-the-country/index.html

- *Brief for appellant - Statutes involved*. (n.d.). Law.jrank.org . https://law.jrank.org/pages/11631/Brief-Appellant-STATUTES-INVOLVED.html

- Brookes, B. (2013). *Abortion in England 1900-1967*. Routledge.

- Brotman, B. (1990, April 8). *Abortion law blamed in death*. Chicago Tribune. https://www.chicagotribune.com/news/ct-xpm-1990-04-08-9001290267-story.html

- Buell, S. (1991). *Criminal abortion revisited*. P

ubMed.gov. https://pubmed.ncbi.nlm.nih.g
ov/11652642/

- Carlson, A. C. (2009). *The crimes of womanhood*. University for Illinois Press.

- *Catechism of the Catholic Church*. (n.d.). Catechism of the Catholic Church - IntraText. vatican.va. https://www.vatican.va/archive/EN G0015/__P7Z.HTM#-2C6

- CBN.com. (2022). *Alveda King: A voice for the voiceless*. CBN - the Christian Broadcasting Network. https://www1.cbn.com/700club/al veda-king-voice-voiceless

- CNA. (2021, October 4). *Pope Francis' 8 strongest statements against abortion*. Catholic News Agency. https://www.catholicnewsagency.com/news/ 249172/pope-francis-abortion-statements

- CNA. (2022, March 4). *Experts respond to Biden: Biology and theology agree, human life begins at conception*. Catholic News Agency. https://www.catholicnewsagency.com/news/ 250572/experts-respond-to-biden-biology -and-theology-agree-human-life-begins-at -conception

- Diamant, J., & Mohamed, B. (2022, June 24). *What the data says about abortion in the U.S.* Pew Research Center. https://www.pewresearch.org/fact-tank/2022/06/24/what-the-data-says-about-abortion-in-the-u-s-2/

- Doan, A. E., (2007). *Opposition & intimidation [electronic resource] : the abortion wars & strategies of political harassment.* Internet Archive. Ann Arbor : University of Michigan Press. https://archive.org/details/oppositionintimi00doan

- Donohue, J. J., & Levitt, S. D. (2019). *The impact of legalized abortion on crime over the last two decades.* SSRN Electronic Journal. https://doi.org/10.2139/ssrn.3391510

- *Early English laws: Leges henrici primi (Hn).* (2022). Earlyenglishlaws.ac.uk. https://earlyenglishlaws.ac.uk/laws/texts/hn/

- Eastside Gynecology. (2019, April 2). *History of abortion in the U.S. timeline | Eastside Gynecology.* Eastside Gynecology. https://eastsidegynecology.com/blog/us-abortion-history-timeline/

-

Editors, H. com. (2022, June 24). *Roe v. Wade.* H I S T O R Y . https://www.history.com/topics/womens-rights/roe-v-wade#abortion-before-roe-v-wade

- Eisenberg, B., & Ruthsdotter, M. (1998). *History of the women's rights movement.* National Women's History Alliance. https://nationalwomenshistoryalliance.org/history-of-the-womens-rights-movement/

- Farrell, M. (2022, May 5). *Ben Franklin put an abortion recipe in his math textbook.* Slate. https://slate.com/news-and-politics/2022/05/ben-franklin-american-instructor-textbook-abortion-recipe.html

- Feiner, L., & Mangan, D. (2022, June 24). *Trump takes credit for end of Roe v. Wade after his 3 Supreme Court justice picks vote to void abortion rights.* CNBC. https://www.cnbc.com/2022/06/24/roe-v-wade-decision-trump-takes-credit-for-supreme-court-abortion-ruling.html

- Figueroa, F. (2022, June 25). *"A real victory for life:" Austin abortion opponents celebrate overturn of Roe v. Wade.* Austin

American-Statesman. https://www.statesman.com/story/news/2022/06/25/overturn-roe-v-wade-celebrated-austin-pro-life-advocates-abortion-opponents/7733995001/

- Garrett, A. (2022, May 3). *Who are the Supreme Court justices who decided Roe v. Wade?* Market Realist. https://marketrealist.com/p/1973-supreme-court-justices/

- Gold, R.B. (2004, September 22). *Lessons from before Roe: Will past be prologue?* Guttmacher Institute. https://www.guttmacher.org/gpr/2003/03/lessons-roe-will-past-be-prologue#

- Green, A. (2022). Sarah Weddington. *The Lancet*, 10330, 1112. https://doi.org/10.1016/S0140-6736(22)00489-5

- Grimes, D. A. (2015, March 17). *The bad old days: Abortion in America before Roe v. Wade.* HuffPost. https://www.huffpost.com/entry/the-bad-old-days-abortion_b_6324610

- Gross, T. (2022, June 23). *Why overturning Roe isn't the final goal of the anti-abortion movement.* N P R .

https://www.npr.org/2022/06/23/110692205
0/why-overturning-roe-isnt-the-final-goal
-of-the-anti-abortion-movement

- Guttmacher Institute. (2019, March 4). *State bans on abortion through-out pregnancy*. Guttmacher Institute. https://www.guttmacher.org/state-poli cy/explore/state-policies-later-abortions

- Guttmacher Institute. (2020, November 6). *Abortion service delivery in clinics by state policy climate in 2017*. Guttmacher Institute. https://www.guttmacher.org/article/2020/1 0/abortion-service-delivery-clinics-state-po licy-climate-2017

- Guttmacher Institute. (2021, April 23). *The Hyde Amendment: A discriminatory ban on insurance coverage of abortion*. Guttmacher Institute. https://www.guttmacher.org/fact-shee t/hyde-amendment

- Harris, J. (2022, June 24). *Anti- and pro-abortion reaction pours in after Roe v. Wade overturned*. News4Jax. https://www.news4jax.com/news/local/2022 /06/24/anti-and-pro-abortion-reaction-pou rs-in-after-roe-v-wade-overturned/

- Harvey-Jenner, C. (2014, October 14). *"Dear Little Thing": One woman's open letter to her aborted child.* Cosmopolitan. https://www.cosmopolitan.com/uk/reports/news/a30400/dear-little-thing-woman-writes-open-letter-abortion/

- Huffman, B. (2017, February 7). *Ginsburg dissent: Gonzales v. Carhart case summary.* UH School of Law Library. https://library.law.hawaii.edu/2017/02/07/ginsburg-dissent-gonzales-v-carhart/

- Isaac, S. (2022, June 24). *Pro-lifers celebrate outside Supreme Court after monumental ruling overturning Roe.* National Review. https://www.nationalreview.com/news/pro-lifers-celebrate-outside-supreme-court-after-monumental-ruling-overturning-roe/

- Joffe, C. E., Weitz, T. A., & Stacey, C. L. (2004). Uneasy allies: pro-choice physicians, feminist health activists and the struggle for abortion rights. *Sociology of health and illness*, 26(6), 775–796. https://doi.org/10.1111/j.0141-9889.2004.00418.x

- Jones, R. K., Zolna, M. R. S., Henshaw, S. K., & Finer, L. B. (2008). Abortion in the United States: Incidence and access to services, 2005. *Perspectives on sexual and reproductive health*, 40(1), 6–16. https://doi.org/10.1363/4 000608

- Karrer, R. N. (2011). The National Right to Life Committee: Its founding, its history, and the emergence of the pro-life movement prior to Roe v. Wade. *The Catholic historical review*, 97(3), 527–557. https://doi.org/10.135 3/cat.2011.0098

- Khan, E. (2019, February 21). *Top 10 countries with highest rape crime - Wonderslist*. WondersList. https://www.wonderslist.com/10-c ountries-highest-rape-crime/

- Lane, M. (2022, July 23). *Mark Lane: "Defend Shirley Wheeler!" '70s Daytona abortion case in the news again*. Daytona Beach News-Journal O   n   l   i   n   e   . https://www.news-journalonline.com/story/ opinion/columns/2022/07/23/shirley-ann -wheeler-florida-1971-abortion-case-again-n ews-billboard/10085079002/

- Lawder, D. (2022, May 10). *Yellen says ending abortion access would be "damaging" to U.S. economy,   women*.   Reuters.

https://www.reuters.com/legal/litigation/yel
len-says-eliminating-abortion-rights-would
-have-damaging-effects-us-economy-2022
-05-10/

- Lehman, C. F. (2020, September 1). *Fewer American high schoolers having sex than ever before.* Institute for Family Studies. https://ifstudies.org/blog/fewer-american-h igh-schoolers-having-sex-than-ever-before

- Luker, K. (1984). *Abortion and the politics of motherhood.* University of California Press.

- Mangan, L. F., Dan. (2022, June 24). *Trump takes credit for end of Roe v. Wade after his 3 Supreme Court justice picks vote to void abortion rights.* CNBC. https://www.cnbc.com/2022/06/24/roe-v-w ade-decision-trump-takes-credit-for-supre me-court-abortion-ruling.html

- Mehta, S. (2022, June 13). *There is no one "religious view" on abortion: A scholar of religion, gender and sexuality explains.* The Conversation. https://theconversation.com/there-is-no-on e-religious-view-on-abortion-a-scholar-of-r

eligion-gender-and-sexuality-explains-1845
32

- Murphy, H. (2017, October 30). *What experts know about men who rape.* The New York Times. https://www.nytimes.com/2017/10/30/health/men-rape-sexual-assault.html

- NARAL Pro-Choice America. (2022, June 24). *NARAL pro-choice America condemns U.S. Supreme Court decision overturning Roe v. Wade.* NARAL Pro-Choice America. https://www.prochoiceamerica.org/2022/06/24/naral-pro-choice-america-condemns-u-s-supreme-court-decision-overturning-roe-v-wade/

- Nguyen, R. (2022, May 22). *We asked readers how Roe v. Wade has affected their lives; Here are their stories.* The Seattle Times. https://www.seattletimes.com/seattle-news/politics/we-asked-readers-how-roe-v-wade-has-affected-their-lives-here-are-your-stories/

- NRLC. (2022). *U.S. abortion statistics by year (1973-Current).* Christian Life Resources. https://christianliferesources.com/2021/01/1

9/u-s-abortion-statistics-by-year-1973-curre nt/

- Paintin, D. (1998). A medical view of abortion in the 1960s. *Abortion Law and Politics Today*, 12–19. https://doi.org/10.1007/978-1-349-26 876-4_2

- Pew Research Centre. (2022, June 23). *A look at the changing number of legal abortions in the U.S. since the 1970s.* Pew Research Center. https://www.pewresearch.org/fact-tank/202 2/06/24/what-the-data-says-about-abortion -in-the-u-s-2/ft_2022-06-23_abortiondata _01/

- Pierson, B., Hals, T., & Thomsen, J. (2022, May 9). *After Roe v Wade, next U.S. abortion battle: state v state.* Reuters https://www.reuters.com/legal/government/ after-roe-v-wade-next-us-abortion-battle-st ate-v-state-2022-05-09/

- Population Resource Bureau. (2021, March). *Abortion facts and figures 2021.* PRB.org. https://www.prb.org/wp-content/uploads/2 021/03/2021-safe-engage-abortion-facts-an d-figures-media-guide.pdf

-

Procon.org. (2019, May 9). *Abortion pros and cons*. ProCon.org. https://abortion.procon.org/

- Quotefancy. (n.d.). *Aristotle quote: "The line between lawful and unlawful abortion will be marked by the fact of having sensation and being alive."* Quotefancy.com. https://quotefancy.com/quote/767430/Aristotle-The-line-between-lawful-and-unlawful-abortion-will-be-marked-by-the-fact-of

- Reagan, L. J. (2008). *When abortion was a crime : women, medicine, and law in the United States, 1867-1973*. University Of California Press.

- *Revolution 1868-1872, The*. (n.d.) Accessible Archives https://www.accessible-archives.com/collections/the-revolution/

- Reynolds-Wright, J. (2013). The moral and philosophical importance of abortion. *Journal of Family Planning and Reproductive Health Care*, 39(1), 51–53. https://doi.org/10.1136/jfprhc-2012-100427

- Ries, J. (2022, May 11). *Ectopic pregnancy and abortion laws: What to know*. Healthline. https://www.healthline.com/health-news/ec

topic-pregnancy-and-abortion-laws-what-to-know

- Rosenberg, E. (2019, May 30). *Clarence Thomas tried to link abortion to eugenics. Seven historians told The Post he's wrong.* Washington Post. https://www.washingtonpost.com/history/2019/05/31/clarence-thomas-tried-link-abortion-eugenics-seven-historians-told-post-hes-wrong/

- Shin, Y., Siegel, R., & Mellnik, T. (2022, June 2). *How women's lives were different before Roe v. Wade.* Washington Post. https://www.washingtonpost.com/business/interactive/2022/women-before-roe-v-wade/

- Silliman, D. (2022, June 24). *Goodbye Roe v. Wade.* Christianity Today. https://www.christianitytoday.com/news/2022/june/roe-v-wade-overturn-abortion-supreme-court-ruling-pro-life.html

- Skerry, P. (1978, July 1). *Abortion in America, by James C. Mohr; The ambivalence of abortion, by Linda Bird Francke.* Commentary Magazine. https://www.commentary.org/articles/peter

-skerry/abortion-in-america-by-james-c-m
ohr-the-ambivalence-of-abortion-by-linda
-bird-francke/

- Snodgrass, E. (2022). *Which Supreme Court justices voted to overturn Roe v. Wade? Here's where all 9 judges stand.* Business Insider. https://www.businessinsider.com/which-supreme-court-justices-voted-to-overturn-roe-v-wade-2022-6

- Soros, G. (2022, July 4). *US democracy under concerted attack.* Project Syndicate. https://www.project-syndicate.org/commentary/radical-supreme-court-undermining-democracy-in-america-by-george-soros-2022-07?utm_medium=ads&utm_source=GoogleSearch&utm_content=OSF&utm_campaign=OpEd

- South Avenue (2020, January 6). *Margaret Sanger and the history of the birth control pill.* South Avenue Women's Services. https://www.southavewomensservices.com/margaret-sanger-and-the-history-of-the-birth-control-pill/

- Staley, T., Guo, J. (2021, November 23). *Dobbs v. Jackson Women's Health Organization.* Legal

Information Institute. https://www.law.corn ell.edu/supct/cert/19-1392

- Statista. (2021). *U.S.: number of rape/sexual assault victims, by sex 2019*. Statista. https://www.statista.com/statistics/251923/u sa--reported-forcible-rape-cases-by-gender /

- Stevenson, A. J. (2021). The pregnancy-related mortality impact of a total abortion ban in the United States: A research note on increased deaths due to remaining pregnant. *Demography*, 58(6). https://doi.org/10.1215/0 0703370-9585908

- Stohr, G. (2022, June 24). *Bloomberg - Are you a robot?* Bloomberg.com. https://www.bloomberg.com/news/articles/ 2022-06-24/supreme-court-overturns-roe -v-wade-abortion-rights-ruling

- Storer, H. R. (1868). *Why not?: A book for every woman.* Lee and Shepard. https://books.google.co.za/books?id=PDEZA AAAYAAJ&printsec=frontcover&source=gbs _ge_summary_r&cad=0#v=onepage&q&f= false

•

Supreme Court; Excerpts from major opinions, The. (1994, April 7). The New York Times. https://www.nytimes.com/1994/04/07/us/th e-supreme-court-excerpts-from-major-opi nions.html#:~:text=We%20need%20not%20r esolve%20the

- Temme Esq., L. (2022, July 6). *Could Roe v. Wade be overturned?* Findlaw. https://supreme.findlaw.com/supreme-cour t-insights/could-roe-v--wade-be-overturne d-.html

- United Nations. (1948, December 10). *Universal Declaration of Human Rights*. United Nations. https://www.un.org/en/about-us/univ ersal-declaration-of-human-rights

- UN Women. (2019). *UN Women - United nations entity for gender equality and the empowerment of women*. UN Women. https://www.un women.org/en

- Wikipedia Contributors. (2019, January 25). *Abortion in the United States*. Wikipedia; Wikimedia Foundation. https://en.wikipedia.org /wiki/Abortion_in_the_United_States

- Wind, R. (2014, February 3). *U.S. abortion rate*

hits lowest level since 1973. Guttmacher I n s t i t u t e . https://www.guttmacher.org/news-release/2 014/us-abortion-rate-hits-lowest-level-1973 #

- World Health Organization. (2021, November 25). *Abortion.* World Health Organization. https://www.who.int/news-room/fa ct-sheets/detail/abortion

Printed in Great Britain
by Amazon

43072864R00106